The Power of the Cross

The Power of the Cross

RANIERO CANTALAMESSA

Translated by
Frances Lonergan Villa

DARTON·LONGMAN + TODD

First published in Great Britain in 1996 by
Darton, Longman and Todd Ltd
1 Spencer Court
140–142 Wandsworth High Street
London SW18 4JJ

Originally published in Italian in 1994 as *Noi Predichiamo Cristo Crocifisso* by Editrice Ancora, Milano

ISBN 0–232–52160–3

A catalogue record for this book is available
from the British Library

Scripture quotations are taken
from the Jerusalem Bible, published and copyright 1966, 1967
and 1968 by Darton, Longman and Todd Ltd and Doubleday
and Co Inc.

Phototypeset by Intype London Ltd
Printed and bound in Great Britain by Page Bros, Norwich

Contents

Introduction

THERE IS A day in the year when, for once, the high point in the liturgy of the Church is not the Eucharist, but the cross; in other words, the liturgy is not centred on the sacrament but on the event. This day is Good Friday, when Mass is not celebrated and we contemplate and adore only the cross.

Although throughout the Easter Vigil the Church commemorates both the death and resurrection of Christ, as two inseparable moments of one Easter mystery, she soon felt the need to dedicate a special day to the passion to show the importance and the infinite richness of that moment in which 'all was accomplished'. From the fourth century onwards, therefore, there have been services for the adoration of the cross on Good Friday, and these were destined to have a very positive influence on the faith and worship of Christians throughout the centuries. There is a special grace passing through the Church on that day. This is the day when 'the mystery of the cross shines out', *fulget crucis mysterium,* as an ancient hymn says.

The meditations in this book were prepared for this time and this atmosphere of commemoration and adoration. They are comments on the Passion readings given in St Peter's Basilica in Rome, in the presence of the pope, during the Good Friday services from 1980 to 1995. The order is the same in which they were delivered, except the one on Jesus the Lord, which was given in 1986, but which has been placed first as something of a key to the whole book.

Together, these meditations form in some measure a prolonged contemplation on the cross and a kind of special 'way of the cross' entirely based on God's word. Sometimes the tone is kerygmatic, like a mighty proclamation of the power of the cross, while at other times it is more moral and devotional.

The book may serve the twofold purpose of meditation on the passion of Christ and input for a new evangelisation, for it is a fact that today, as in the early Church, the Gospel will not make headway in the world through 'the wisdom of discourses' but through the mysterious power of the cross. St Paul said, 'While the Jews demand miracles and the Greeks look for wisdom, here are we preaching a crucified Christ; to the Jews an obstacle that they cannot get over, to the pagans madness, but to those who have been called, whether they are Jews or Greeks, a Christ who is the power and the wisdom of God' (1 Co 1:22–24). This book is just a simple echo of these words which still retain all their original significance.

1

Let every tongue proclaim that Jesus Christ is Lord!

ON THE DAY of Yom Kippur, the holiest day of the year for the Jews, the Day of Atonement, the high priest, carrying the blood of the sacrifice, went through the temple curtain and entered the Holy of Holies and there, alone in the presence of the Most High, he pronounced the divine name. This was the name revealed to Moses by the burning bush. It consisted of four letters, and was so sacred that it was never spoken at any other time, the word 'Adonai', which means 'Lord', being substituted when Scripture was read. I too shall refrain from pronouncing it to respect the tradition of the Jewish people for whom the Church prays on Good Friday. But when it was pronounced in the Holy of Holies it became a link between heaven and earth; it made God present; it atoned for the nation's sins.

Christians also have their Yom Kippur, their Day of Atonement, and this is what we are celebrating. The fulfilment was proclaimed in the second reading of this liturgical service, which was taken from the Epistle to the Hebrews, 'In Jesus, the Son of God, we have the supreme high priest who has gone through to the highest heaven' (Heb 4:14). The same Letter tells us that Christ 'entered the sanctuary once and for all, taking with him not the blood of goats and bull calves, but his own blood' (Heb 9:12). Today as we celebrate the Great Atonement, no longer figuratively but in reality, no longer for the sins of one nation but for 'the sins of the whole world' (1 Jn 2:2; Rm 3:25), a Name is proclaimed. In the acclamation before the gospel these words taken from St Paul were sung: 'Christ became obedient unto death, even death on a cross. Therefore God has highly exalted him and bestowed on him the Name which is above every name.' The apostle also refrains from pronouncing this ineffable name, substituting it with *Adonai*, in Greek *Kyrios*, *Dominus* in Latin and *Lord* in English. The reading then continues, 'So that all beings . . . should bend the knee at the name of Jesus and that every tongue should acclaim Jesus Christ as Lord, to the glory of God the Father' (Ph 2:8–11). By the word 'Lord', he means precisely the name that proclaims the divine being. The Father gave Christ – also as man – his own name and authority (Mt 28:18). This is the unprecedented truth contained in the proclamation, 'Jesus Christ is Lord!' Jesus Christ is the 'I Am', the Living One.

It is not only St Paul who proclaims this truth. In John's gospel Jesus says, 'When you have lifted up the Son of Man, then you will know that I am He' (Jn 8:28). And again he says, 'You will die in your sins if you do not believe that I am He' (Jn 8:24). Now the remission of sins takes place in this name, in this person. We have just heard in the reading of the passion what happened when the soldiers went to take Jesus: 'Who are you looking for?' Jesus asked them and they answered him, 'Jesus the Nazarene'. Jesus said to them, 'I am he', and they drew back and fell to the ground (Jn 18:4–6). Why did they fall to the ground? Because he had pronounced his divine name,

Ego eimi, 'I am he', and for an instant this name was free to reveal its authority. For John the Evangelist too, the divine name is closely linked to the obedience of Jesus unto death, 'When you have lifted up the Son of Man, then you will know that I am He and that I do nothing of myself: what the Father has taught me is what I preach' (Jn 8:28). Jesus is not Lord against the Father or in the Father's place, but to 'the glory of God the Father'.

* * *

This is the faith the Church inherited from the apostles and which sanctified her beginnings and formed her worship and even her art. On the halo of Christ Pantocrator in ancient mosaics and icons there are three Greek letters inscribed in gold, *O ŌN*, 'He who is'. We are here to revive this faith, even out of the very stones if necessary. During the first centuries of the Church, in the week after baptism, usually Easter week, the most sacred truths of the Christian faith were revealed and entrusted to the neophytes. Before this, following the so-called 'Discipline of the secret' (*Disciplina arcani*) then in force, they were kept hidden or at best only alluded to. Day after day the 'mysteries' were unfolded to the neophytes: baptism, the Eucharist, the Our Father, and their symbolism, which gave it the name of 'mystagogic catechesis'. It was a unique experience, the greatness of the spiritual truths opening before their eyes leaving a lasting impression on them. Tertullian said that the converts 'were startled by the revelation of these truths' (*Apologeticum* 39, 9).

Today all this has changed but the liturgy still offers us occasions to recreate such moments, and this Good Friday solemn liturgy is one of them. This evening, if we concentrate on it, the Church has something to reveal and hand down to us as it did to the neophytes. It has the Lordship of Christ to hand down to us. It has the hidden secret to reveal to us that 'Jesus is Lord' and that every knee must bow before him; that one day every knee will unfailingly 'bow before him'! (Is 45:23). In the Old Testament it is said that 'the Lord has launched a word at Jacob and it has fallen on Israel (Is 9:7)'. Now these words 'Jesus is Lord', the greatest of all words, are 'hurled' at us, and 'fall' upon this congregation, they become a living reality for us right here in the very heart of the Catholic Church. They pass among us like the flaming torch between the victims prepared by Abraham for the sacrifice of the convenant (Gn 15:17).

'Lord' is the divine name that concerns us most directly. God was 'God' and 'Father' before the existence of the world, the angels and man, but he was not yet 'Lord'. He became Lord, *Dominus*, the moment creatures existed over which to exercise his dominion and which freely accepted his dominion. In the Trinity there are no 'lords' as there are no servants, and all three persons are equal. In a certain sense we make God 'Lord'!

God's dominion, rejected by sin, was re-established by Christ, the new Adam. In Christ, God has become Lord again by an even greater right, that is, not only by creation but also by redemption. God reigns again from the cross! *Regnavit a ligno Deus*. 'This explains why Christ both died and came to life, it was so that he might be Lord both of the dead and of the living' (Rm 14:9).

* * *

The *objective dimension* of the words 'Jesus is Lord' lies in the fact that it makes history present. It is the conclusion of two fundamental events: Jesus died for our sins; he is risen for our justification: therefore Jesus is lord! The events which led up to it are, so to speak, contained in the conclusion and become present and operative in it when we confess in faith. 'If your lips confess that Jesus is Lord and if you believe in your heart that God raised him from the dead, then you will be saved' (Rm 10:9).

We can participate in the events of salvation in two fundamental ways, through the sacraments and the word. Here we mean the word in its most sublime form, the *kerygma*. Christianity is rich in examples and models of experiences of the divine. Orthodox spirituality stresses the experience of God through the 'mysteries', through prayer of the heart. Western spirituality stresses the experience of God through contemplation, when the soul recollects itself and the mind rises beyond itself and earthly things. There are, in fact, many 'journeys of the soul to God'. But God's word reveals a way that opened the horizon of God to the first Christians, a way that is not extraordinary, and neither is it reserved to a privileged few but is possible to all men of upright heart, to those who believe and to those in search of faith; it does not ascend through stages of contemplation but through the divine events of salvation; it does not come from silence but from listening, and this is the way of the kerygma: 'Christ has died! Christ is risen! Christ is Lord'.

Perhaps the first Christians experienced something similar when they exclaimed '*Maranatha*' during worship. This had two meanings depending on the way it was pronounced. It could mean either 'Come, Lord!' or 'The Lord has come'. It could express a yearning for Christ's return or a joyous response to his manifestation to the congregation in prayer.

The awareness of the risen Lord's presence is a sort of inner illumination that can provoke a complete change of heart. It recalls what happened when the risen Christ appeared to his disciples. One day after Easter the apostles

[7]

were fishing by the Sea of Galilee when a man stood on the beach and spoke to them. Everything was quite normal; they were complaining that they had caught nothing. But then, unexpectedly, the disciple that Jesus loved in a flash of recognition exclaimed, 'It is the Lord,' and immediately the situation on the boat changed.

We can see now why St Paul claims that 'No one can say, "Jesus is Lord" unless he is under the influence of the Holy Spirit' (1 Co 12:3). Just as the bread on the altar becomes the living body of Christ by the power of the Holy Spirit descending upon it, so these words become 'alive and active' (Heb 4:12) by the power of the Holy Spirit operating in them. It is an event of grace that we can predispose, favour and desire but which we cannot ourselves cause. It is usually afterwards, maybe even years later, that we become aware of what has happened. At this moment, what took place in the heart of the much-loved disciple on the Sea of Galilee could be taking place in the heart of someone present here; someone could be 'acknowledging' the Lord.

* * *

There is also a *subjective dimension* in the words 'Jesus is Lord!' which depends on the person saying them. I have often wondered why the demons in the gospels never once gave Jesus this title. They go as far as saying, 'You are the Son of God', or 'You are the Holy one of God!' (Mt 4:3; Mk 3:11, 5:7; Lk 4:41); but they never say, 'You are the Lord!' The most plausible reason for this seems that to say, 'You are the Son of God' is to simply acknowledge a given fact which does not depend on them and which they cannot change. They know that Jesus is God's Son. (Some theologians today don't know it, but the demons do.) But to say, 'You are the Lord!' is a different matter. It means to recognise him as such and to submit to his Lordship. If the demons were to do so they would immediately cease to be what they are and become angels of light again.

These words divide two worlds. To say, 'Jesus is Lord!' means to freely enter his dominion. It is like saying, 'Jesus Christ is *my* Lord, the very reason of my existence. I live for him and no longer for myself.' St Paul wrote to the Romans, 'The life and death of each of us has its influence on others; if we live, we live for the Lord; and if we die, we die for the Lord, so that alive or dead we belong to the Lord' (Rm 14:7–8). The greatest contradiction, that between life and death and ever present in man, has been overcome. Now the radical contradiction is no longer between living and dying but between living 'for the Lord' and living for oneself. Living for oneself is the new name for death.

After Easter the proclamation, 'Jesus is Lord!' substituted the proclamation of the historical Jesus, 'The kingdom of God has come to you.' Before the gospels were written, and even before they were planned, the news existed that 'Jesus is risen. He is the Messiah. He is the Lord!' It all started here. Like a seed, this news contained all the authority of evangelical teaching and from that seed came the majestic tree of all the teaching and theology of the Church. However, as happens with natural seed, it has remained buried beneath the plant it produced. To our minds today the kerygma is a truth of the faith, a point, however important, of teaching and preaching. It no longer stands out as the very origin of the faith.

My first reaction to a Scripture text is always to seek the resonances it has in tradition, that is, in the Fathers of the Church, the liturgy and the saints. Usually testimonies come teeming into my mind, but with the words, 'Jesus is Lord!' I was forced to admit that there is almost no mention of it in tradition. In the third century AD the original meaning of 'Lord' had already been lost sight of. It was considered a proper title for those who were still 'servants' and not yet 'friends'. It therefore corresponded to a state of fear, not love (Origen, *Commentary on the Gospel of John*, I, 29), whereas we know it is a different thing altogether.

For a new worldwide evangelisation we must again bring to light that seed which holds the whole Christian message. It is necessary to unearth 'the sword of the Spirit', the impassioned message of the Lord Jesus. A well-known epic cycle of medieval Christendom, concerning the Knights of the Round Table, tells of a world where everything languishes in confusion because no one any longer asks the essential question: 'Where is the Holy Grail?' but where everything reflourishes once these sacred words are pronounced again and dominate anew every thought. I am convinced that something similar is happening as regards the kerygma 'Jesus is Lord!' Everything languishes and lacks vigour where these words are no longer proclaimed, or are no longer proclaimed 'in the Spirit'; but where they are pronounced in all their purity and faith everything is reanimated and revives. Nothing is more familiar to us than the word 'Lord'. It is part of the very name which concludes every liturgical prayer. However, it is one thing to say 'Our Lord Jesus Christ' and another to say 'Jesus Christ is our Lord!' For centuries the proclamation 'Jesus is Lord' in Philippians 2:11 has been blurred by a bad translation. In fact, the meaning of this famous passage is not 'the Lord Jesus Christ is in the glory of God the Father', as the Vulgate said, but 'Jesus Christ is Lord, to the glory of God the Father'.

* * *

Yet it is not sufficient to proclaim verbally that Jesus Christ is Lord; it is also necessary that 'every knee shall bend'. These are not two separate things. Whoever proclaims Jesus as Lord must bend his knee in doing so. He must, as it were, lovingly submit himself to the reality, bending his intelligence in obedience to faith. It is a question of renouncing that feeling of power and security that comes from 'wisdom', that is, from the ability to face this incredulous and proud world of ours with its own weapons of dialectics, endless arguments and discussions. All of this allows us to 'endlessly seek learning but never reach knowledge' (2 Tm 3:7), and therefore never be compelled to obey the truth once it has been discovered. The kerygma offers no explanations but exacts obedience because in it God's own authority is at work. *After* it and *beside* it we can give all the reasons and demonstrations we like, but not *within* it. The light of the sun is in the sun, and as it illuminates everything, it cannot itself be illuminated. One has to be blind not to see it.

We must accept the 'weaknesses' and 'foolishness' of the kerygma – and this means we accept our own weaknesses, humiliations and defeats – to allow God's power and wisdom to triumph again. St Paul says, 'Our war is not fought with weapons of flesh, yet they are strong enough, in God's cause, to demolish fortresses. We demolish sophistries, and the arrogance that tries to resist the knowledge of God; every thought is our prisoner, captured to be brought into obedience to Christ' (2 Co 10:4–5). In other words, we must stay on the cross, as that is where the power of the Lordship of Christ comes to us.

We must be careful not to be ashamed of the kerygma, for there is such a temptation. Even Paul felt it and to himself cried out, 'I am not ashamed of the Good News!' (Rm 1:16). The temptation is even stronger today. We

[11]

wonder what sense there is in talking about the risen Christ who is Lord when, around us, we see the numerous real problems that assail man: hunger, injustice, war. Man delights in hearing himself talked about, whether good or bad, much more than hearing God talked about. In Paul's time, part of the world looked for miracles and another part for wisdom. Today, part looks for justice (those living under capitalist regimes) and another part looks for freedom (those living under Communist regimes). But we preach Jesus Christ crucified and risen (1 Co 1:23), for we are convinced that the foundation of true justice and freedom are to be found in him.

* * *

In mystagogic catechesis the mysteries were revealed by word and by rite. The neophytes heard the mysteries explained and attended the rites, especially the eucharistic rite, which they had never previously seen with their own eyes. Something similar is taking place in this service where the mystery of the Lordship of Christ is being entrusted to us. After the liturgy of the word, the rite will follow. The cross will solemnly be unveiled and we shall all genuflect three times, thus visibly demonstrating that in the Church every knee does bow. The purple veil that has been covering the cross until now is a symbol of the veil that covers the bare cross from the eyes of the world. 'Even today', wrote St Paul, speaking of his fellow-countrymen, 'whenever Moses is read, the veil is over their minds. It will not be removed until they turn to the Lord' (2 Co 3:15–16). Unfortunately, the eyes of many Christians are also covered by that veil, and it will only be removed when 'they turn to the Lord', when they discover the Lordship of Christ. Only then.

This evening, when the bare cross is lifted up before our

eyes, let us gaze upon it. This is the Jesus we proclaim as Lord, not a different one, an easy, rose-water Jesus. What we are about to do is very important. To give us the privilege of calling him King and Lord, as we shall now do, Jesus accepted being called King in mockery; to give us the privilege of humbly bowing our knee before him, he allowed others to kneel before him in derision. It is written: 'The soldiers . . . dressed him up in purple, twisting some thorns and plaiting them into a crown and put it on him. And they began saluting him. . . . They struck his head with a reed, and spat on him; and they went down on their knees to do him homage' (Mk 15: 16–19). We must comprehend well what we are doing so as to act in profound adoration and gratitude, for the price he paid is too high for anything less. Alive, he only heard 'proclamations' of hatred; the 'genuflections' he received were those of ignominy; so let us not add to this with our indifference and superficiality. When he was dying on the cross he could still hear the deafening echoes of the shouting and the word 'King' hung over his head like a sentence. Now that he is at the right hand of the Father and is present among us in the Spirit, let him see that every knee does in fact bow before him, and with it the mind, the heart, the will and everything. Let him hear this cry of joy bursting from the hearts of the redeemed: 'Jesus Christ is the Lord, to the glory of God the Father!'

2

God so loved the world

THE ACCOUNTS OF the Passion, especially in the Synoptic Gospels, so spare in style and thoroughly lacking in any theological or edifying comment, take us back to the early days of the Church. To use the modern language of 'form criticism', these were the first sections of the gospels to be 'formed' in the oral tradition and circulate among Christians. In this phase, facts are the predominant factor; everything can be summarised in two events: death and resurrection. However, this stage quickly passed. Believers soon queried the 'why' of the Passion. Why did Jesus suffer? And the answer was, 'for our sins!' Thus the Easter faith began, expressed by St Paul in his well-known formula, 'Jesus, who was put to death for our sins and raised to life to justify us' (Rm 4:25). We now had both the facts – death and resurrection – and their significance for us: for our sins, for our justification. The answer seemed complete; history and faith finally formed one Easter mystery.

Instead, the root of the question had not been reached. The query arose again in another form: why did he die for our sins? The answer was like a flash of sunlight illuminating the faith of the Church, 'because he loved us!' He loved you, giving himself up in our place' (Ep 5:2); 'the Son of God who loved me and who sacrificed himself for my sake' (Ga 2:20); 'Christ loved the Church and sacri-

ficed himself for her' (Ep 5:25). It is an indisputable, primordial truth pervading everything and it applies both to
the Church as a whole and to every individual. St John the
Evangelist, the last to write his gospel, dates this revelation
back to Christ when he was on earth. 'A man can have no
greater love than to lay down his life for his friends. You
are my friends' (Jn 15:13–14).

This answer to the 'why' of Christ's passion is really final
and allows no further questions. He loved us because he
loved us, that's all there is to it! In fact, there is no 'why' to
God's love, it is a free gift. It is the only love in the world
that is truly and totally free, that asks nothing for itself (he
already has everything!) but only gives. Or rather, he gives
himself. 'This is the love I mean; not our love for God, but
God's love for us . . . because he loved us first' (1 Jn 4:10,
19).

Jesus, then, suffered and died freely, out of love. Not by
chance, not from necessity, not because of any obscure
forces or historical reasons overwhelming him unaware or
against his will. If anyone asserts this they are nullifying
the Gospel, removing its soul. Because the Gospel is
nothing other than the good news of God's love in Christ
Jesus. Not only the Gospel but the entire Bible is nothing
other than the news of God's mysterious, incomprehensible love for people. If the whole of Scripture were to start
talking at once, if by some miracle the written words were
transformed into speech, that voice would be more powerful than the waves of the sea, and it would cry out: 'God
loves you!'

* * *

God's love for people has its roots in eternity ('He chose
us in Christ before the world was made', says Paul in Ep
1:4) but was manifested in time, in a series of actual

gestures that make up the history of salvation. In ancient times, God had frequently spoken to the Fathers in many and varied ways about this love of his (Heb 1:1). He had spoken by creating us, because what is creation if not an act of love, the primordial act of God's love for humanity? ('You created the world to fill your creatures with every blessing', we pray in *Eucharistic Prayer IV.*) Later, he spoke through the prophets, because in reality the biblical prophets are nothing other than messengers of God's love, 'friends of the Bridegroom'. Even their rebukes and threats are intended as a defence of that love of God for his people. In the prophets, God compares his love to that of a mother (Is 49:15ff.) to that of a father (Ho 11:4), to that of a bridegroom (Is 62:5). God himself sums up his whole behaviour towards Israel by saying: 'I have loved you with an everlasting love' (Jr 31:3). A phrase unheard of in any philosophy or any religion, on the lips of a god! The 'god of the philosophers' is a God to be loved, not a God who loves, and who loves first.

But it was not enough for God to tell us about his love 'through the prophets'. 'In our time, the last days, he has spoken to us through his Son' (Heb 1:2). There is now an enormous difference, compared with before: Jesus does not confine himself to speaking about God's love, as the prophets did: he *is* the love of God. Because 'God is love', and Jesus is God!

* * *

In Jesus, God no longer speaks to us from a distance, through intermediaries, but from nearby, and in person. He speaks to us from within our human condition, after having savoured to the full the suffering it involves. God's love has become flesh, and has come to live among us! Already in ancient times there were those who read John

[16]

1:14 in this way. Jesus has loved us with a heart that is at once human and divine, in a perfectly human way, even if the measure of that love is divine. He has loved us with a love that is strong and tender, gentle and constant. How he loves the disciples, how he loves children, how he loves the poor and the sick, how he loves sinners! By loving people, he makes them grow, he restores dignity and hope. All who draw near to Jesus with a simple heart emerge transformed by his love.

His love turns to friendship: 'I no longer call you serv-ants, but friends' (Jn 15:15). But he does not stop there: he even goes to the point of identifying with humanity, so that human analogies, even that of a mother, a father or a spouse are no longer enough: 'Remain in me', he says, 'as I remain in you.'

Finally, we have the supreme test of this love: 'He had always loved those who were his in the world, but now he showed how perfect his love was' (Jn 13:1), in other words, he loved to the extreme limit of love. Two things reveal the true lover and make love triumph: the first consists in doing good to the beloved, the second (by far superior) in suffering for him or her. This is why, in order to prove his great love for us, God finds a way of bringing about his own annihilation, and achieves it in such a way that he is able to endure terrible sufferings. In this way, through all that he endures, God convinces men and women of his extraordinary love for them and once again draws to himself the very people who had fled from the good Lord, thinking that they were the objects of his hatred (N. Cabasilas, *Vita in Cristo*, VI, 2). Jesus repeats to us what he once said to a saint who was meditating on the passion: 'My love for you was not a joke'! (Blessed Angela of Foligno).

If we want to know how much God loved us, we have a

simple and certain way of knowing: by looking at how much he suffered! Not just in his body but most of all in his soul. Because the true passion of Jesus is the one that cannot be seen, the one that made him cry out in Gethsemane, 'My soul is sorrowful to the point of death' (Mk 14:34). Jesus died in his heart before he died physically. Who can fathom the depths of dereliction, sadness and anguish in Christ's soul as he felt himself 'made sin', he who was the innocent Son of the Father? The Good Friday liturgy has rightly placed on Christ's lips the words of the Lamentation: 'All you who pass by this way, look and see: is any sorrow like the sorrow inflicted on me?'

It was with this moment in mind that the words *Sic Deus dilexit mundum* were written ('God loved the world so much' – Jn 3:16). At the beginning of his gospel John exclaims: 'We saw his glory!' (Jn 1:14). If we ask the evangelist, 'Where did you see his glory?' he will reply, 'I saw his glory at the foot of the cross!' Because God's glory lies in the fact that he hid his glory for our sake, that he loved us. This is the greatest glory God has outside of himself, outside of the Trinity, greater even than having created us or having created the entire universe. Seated now at the Father's right hand in glory, Christ's body no longer retains the signs and characteristics of his mortal condition. But the Book of Revelation tells us that there is one thing he does jealously retain and show to the whole court of heaven: his wounds, the signs of his passion. Of these he is proud, because they are the signs of his great love for his creatures.

From the height of the cross, Jesus has reason to repeat to us today, in the words of the liturgy: 'My people, what more could I have done for you that I have not done? Answer me!'

* * *

Someone could say: 'Yes, it's true that Jesus once loved us, when he was on earth, but now? Now that he is no longer among us, what is there left of that love of his, except a faint memory?' The disciples of Emmaus said: 'Three days have already gone by', and we are tempted to say: 'Two thousand years have already gone by!' But they were wrong, because Jesus was risen and was walking by their side! Just as we are wrong when we think like them, in fact his love is still among us because 'the love of God has been poured into our hearts by the Holy Spirit which has been given to us' (Rm 5:5). And here is the second great truth we celebrate today, no less beautiful and important than the first: God loved the world so much that he gave us the Holy Spirit! The water flowing from Christ's side, together with the blood, was the symbol of the Holy Spirit. 'We can know that we are living in him and he is living in us because he lets us share his Spirit' (1 Jn 4:13). Let us remember this phrase of John's – it sums up everything. It means that Jesus has left us as a gift his whole self, whole love, because 'in the Spirit he was raised to life' (1 P 3:18).

* * *

What I have just described is the objective revelation of God's love in history. Let us now think of ourselves. What shall we do and say after listening to the extent of God's love for us? There are several possible responses, and one of them is to return God's love! This is the first and great-est commandment of the law! An ancient Church hymn says; 'How can we not love one who has so loved us?' (*Sic nos amantem quis non redamaret?*) However, there is something else to do first.

Another possible answer is to love one another as God loved us! Doesn't John the Evangelist tell us that if God loved us, 'we too should love one another' (1 Jn

4:11)? But even before this there is something else. First of all we must believe in God's love! 'We ourselves have known and put our faith in God's love towards ourselves' (1 Jn 4:16). It is not faith as a simple intellectual assent to a truth. It is much more; it is amazed faith, *incredulous* faith (indeed a paradox!); such faith that, even while believing, one cannot convince oneself of what one believes. How could it possibly be that God, infinitely happy in his quiet eternity, desired not only to create us but to personally come and suffer among us? How can this be true? Most of the New Testament quotations cited so far are exclamations; they express the sense of awe of the early Church: 'He loved me and he gave himself for me!' 'God so loved the world!'

What a marvel this faith is, made up of awe and admiration, yet more difficult than anything else could ever be. Do we really believe that God loves us? No, we don't really believe it, or at least not strongly enough! And if we were to believe it, everything, our lives, ourselves, things and events would be transfigured before our eyes. This very day we would be in paradise with him, for paradise is simply rejoicing in God's love. An extra-canonical saying attributed to Jesus says, 'Whoever is amazed will reign.' And this is the realisation of these words. Whoever, before God's unbelievable love for us, is seized with a profound sense of awe, whoever remains speechless before this love, will immediately enter the Kingdom of Heaven!

But, as I have said, we really don't believe that God loves us; it is ever more difficult to believe in love in this world. There is too much unfaithfulness, too many disappointments. Anyone who has been betrayed or hurt once, is afraid to love again and be loved, because he knows how much pain another betrayal would mean. And so the numbers of those unable to believe in God's love, or rather, in any love, go on increasing. The world and life are falling back into an Ice Age. The earth remains, as Dante says, 'that flower-bed which makes us so ferocious' (*Paradiso* XXII, 151).

Then on a personal level our own unworthiness tempts us: 'It is true that God's love is a beautiful thing, but it's not for me! How could God love anyone as unfaithful and negligent as I am? I am not worthy.' But let us listen to what God says to us: 'Whenever our hearts condemn us, God is greater than our hearts' (1 Jn 3:19ff).

* * *

The world needs to believe in God's love. We must therefore start again to proclaim the gospel of God's love in Jesus Christ. If we don't do so, we shall be like men who place 'their lights under a bushel'. We shall be defrauding the world of its most secret expectation. There are others in the world besides Christians who preach about social justice and respect for man; but there is no one, and I repeat no one, among philosophers or other religions, who tells man that God loves him and loved him first. Yet it is this truth that sustains everything, it is the motive power behind everything. Even the cause of the poor and oppressed is a lost cause if it is not based on the unshakeable truth that God loves us and that he loves the poor and the oppressed.

However, words and sentiments are not enough. Like Jesus, we must be ready to suffer and forgive those that cause suffering. 'Father, forgive them . . .' Jesus uttered these words on the cross and he left them to us Christians so that we would keep them alive, throughout the centuries, and arm ourselves with them. And these words were not intended simply to forgive the enemies Jesus had at that time and who are no longer alive, but to forgive his enemies today, our enemies, the enemies of the Church. Christianity is the religion of forgiving enemies! Only when God's love has helped a man to forgive an enemy at least once, can that man claim to know God's love which was poured into his heart by the Holy Spirit. We should publicly thank those brothers in faith who, when touched by hatred or violent murder, humbly followed the impulse of the Holy Spirit to forgive, even publicly, those who had murdered their dear ones. They believe in love! They have been splendid witnesses in showing that Christ's love, manifest to us on the cross today, is still possible in the Spirit and that only this love can bring about a change in the world because it changes hearts.

So then, I have responded to the prophet Isaiah's cry, ' "Console my people, console them" says your God, "speak to the heart of Jerusalem and call to her that her time of service is ended" ' (Is 40:1–2). I too have dared to speak 'to the heart of Jerusalem', that is, to the Church, to remind her of her most precious possession, the eternal love of her divine Spouse. Now the Spouse himself talks to the Church through the words of the Canticle,

> Arise, my love, my fair one,
> and come away;
> For lo, the winter is past,
> the rain is over and gone.
> The flowers appear on the earth,
> the time of singing has come. (Cant. 2: 10–12)

On the blessed day of Christ's death, a breath of joy uplifts the world.

3

You have killed Jesus of Nazareth!

ON THE DAY of Pentecost, Peter stood up with the other eleven apostles and spoke to the people. What he said can be summarised in a few words, but these few words are as powerful as a clash of thunder: 'You crucified Jesus of Nazareth! God raised him up! Repent!' (Acts 2:23ff).

I wish to make these words live again for us in the hope that they will pierce our hearts as they pierced the hearts of those who were listening to the apostle. The three thousand to whom Peter addressed these words were certainly not all present on Calvary hammering in the nails. Perhaps they were not even present in Pilate's praetorium shouting, '*Crucifige!*' How, then, did they kill Jesus? Because they belonged to the people that killed him. Because they had not listened to the news Jesus brought them, 'The Kingdom of God has come, convert and believe in the Gospel!' Because, perhaps, when Jesus walked the streets of Jerusalem, they had lowered the blinds of their shops so as not to be disturbed.

We know of these things, but we still feel safe enough. We think it doesn't concern us – it concerns those who lived in Palestine in Jesus's time. We are like King David who, hearing the prophet Nathan's account of the great sin committed in the town, finally exploded in anger. 'The man who did this deserves to die!' (2 S 12:5). In the years following the Second World War there was passionate interest in the question of who was responsible for Christ's death, partly due to the Holocaust the Jews had recently experienced. There were numerous books and articles on Christ's trial. The consequences of the answers given to that question were enormous, largely because Christians were participating in the struggle for freedom in various parts of the world. The question of Christ's death became essentially historical and, as such, neutral. In other words, it interests us indirectly because of the consequences today, but not directly as we are not to blame. At any rate, we do not stand as the accused but as the accusers. Some place the blame for the death of Jesus on the religious power of the time, that is, on the Jews; others blame it on the political power, that is, on the Romans, thus making Jesus a martyr in the cause of freedom; and others blame it on both together. It is like a trial where each one more or less consciously repeats to himself what Pilate said: 'I am innocent of this man's blood!' (Mt 27:24).

But what did the prophet Nathan answer to David that day? Pointing to him, he said, 'You are that man!' God cries out the same words to us as we try to discover who killed Jesus: 'You are that man! You killed Jesus of Nazareth! You were there that day; you shouted with the crowd, "Take him away and crucify him!" You were there with Peter when he denied him, with Judas when he betrayed him; you were there with the soldiers when they scourged him, you added your thorn to his crown of thorns, you spat in his face!' The certainty that 'Jesus was put to death for our sins' (Rm 4:25) is at the very heart of our faith. The prophet Isaiah anticipated this truth in a most dramatic way:

[24]

And yet ours were the sufferings he bore,
ours the sorrows he carried . . .
Yet he was pierced through for our faults,
crushed for our sins.
On him lies a punishment that brings us peace,
and through his wounds we are healed (Is 53: 4–5).

We are all accused of his death for we have all sinned,
and it would be a lie to deny this. But is it not the same
thing to say, 'Jesus died for our sins', as to say, 'we killed
Jesus'? The Epistle to the Hebrews says of those who sin
after baptism (that is to say, us) that they 'have wilfully
crucified the Son of God and openly mocked him' (Heb
6:6).

On hearing the terrible accusation, 'You killed Jesus of
Nazareth!' the three thousand were cut to the heart and
said to Peter and the other apostles, 'What must we do,
brothers?' (Acts 2:37). A great fear came upon them, and
it is coming upon us now too, if we are not made of stone.
How could we not be terrified at the thought that God so
loved the world as to give his only Son and we, in answer,
killed him! We have killed life.

It is necessary to experience this inner crisis, the 'fear
and trembling', to become mature Christians and not
remain just Christians in embryo, on the way to light.
Until you have felt lost at least once, worthy of punishment, shipwrecked, you cannot realise what it means to be
saved by Christ's blood; you cannot really know what you
are saying when you call Jesus your 'saviour'. Strictly
speaking, you cannot realise what Jesus suffered and weep
over it. It would be hypocrisy because only he who is inti-
mately convinced that he caused Christ's suffering, that he
inflicted it, really knows what these sufferings were. Jesus
could say to you what he said to the holy women, 'Do not

[25]

weep for me, but weep for yourselves and your sins!' (Lk 23:28).

* * *

There are two possible solutions to a crisis like this: that of Judas, when he cried, 'I have sinned in betraying innocent blood', and went out and hanged himself (Mt 27:4 ff), or Peter's when he went out and 'wept bitterly' (Mt 26:75). Having experienced the power of repentance, Peter can now show the brethren this way of salvation and resolutely cry out to them, 'Repent!'

But what does the word 'repent' mean? How is it realised? It is realised by passing from the state of the *imputation* of sin to the state of the *confession* of sin; from listening to someone else saying to you, 'You killed Jesus of Nazareth!' to you yourself saying in all sincerity and heartfelt sorrow, 'Yes, I killed Jesus of Nazareth!' This passing does not depend only on us; it is the work of the Holy Spirit who 'convinces the world of sin' (Jn 16:8). It is something miraculous. When it happens, man's heart spiritually undergoes the same phenomena that nature underwent that day. The veil covering his mind is torn, his heart of stone is broken, the sepulchre where sin keeps him imprisoned opens; he is finally free. He is born to life again.

What a wonderful thing and worthy of man is confession of sin when it is sincere and free! It permits God to be himself, as it were, 'the God who forgives sin' (Mi 7:18). Siding with God against himself, man induces God to do the same: to side with man against himself and against his own justice. This is obviously out of mercy and not out of need. In fact, God wants to be merciful to the world, but he can't be so if man denies his sin, the very object of God's mercy. The most difficult thing for God to obtain is a 'contrite and humble heart'. His omnipotence is not sufficient for this, he needs our free response. And that is why it is so precious and touches God's heart.

> Thus says the Lord:
> With heaven my throne
> and earth my footstool
> what house could you build me,
> what place for me to rest? . . .
> But my eyes are drawn to the man
> of humbled and contrite spirit. (Is 66: 1–2)

Our misfortune is that we do not truly acknowledge our sin at the very bottom of our hearts. We say, 'After all, what evil have I done?' But, my brother, listen to me, because now I'm going to speak to my own sinful heart, and also to yours. Can't you see your sin? Know then that your sin is precisely that you can't see it! Your sin is self-righteousness; it is the irremediable feeling that your conscience is clear with God and with yourself, even when you call yourself a sinner. This was the sin that led Jesus to the cross for having strongly denounced it among the pharisees.

Feeling yourself righteous, you can no longer understand Christ's cross nor your own cross. You feel that you yourself and the whole world are victims of a disproportionate suffering, too great not to accuse God who permits it. Oh, if we could understand just once what Scripture says, 'since he takes no pleasure in abasing and afflicting the human race' (Lm 3:33), and before the misfortune of his people, his heart recoils within him and his compassion grows warm and tender (Ho 11:8). Then our reaction would be very different. We would exclaim instead, 'Forgive us, Father, if we have compelled you by our sins to treat your beloved Son so harshly. Forgive us if we now compel you to afflict us too, in order to save us, whereas you, like every father, and infinitely more so, wish to give only "good things" to your children! Forgive us if we compel you to deprive yourself of the joy of giving us now, in this world, the happiness for which you made us.'

When I was a boy, I once disobeyed my father by going barefoot somewhere he had told me not to go. A big piece of glass cut my foot. It was during the war, and my poor father had to run considerable risks to get me to the nearest doctor of the allied forces. While the doctor was removing the glass from my foot and dressing the wound, my father stood wringing his hands and he turned away so as not to see. What kind of son would I have been if, once back home, I had accused him of letting me suffer so much without intervening? And yet, that's exactly what we do with God most of the time.

The truth is something else, therefore. We make God suffer, and not the other way round. But we have twisted this truth to the point of asking ourselves after each calamity, 'Where is God? How can God allow all of this?' It is true that God could save us without the cross, but this would be something quite different, and he knows that one day we would be ashamed of having been saved like this, passively, without having been able to collaborate in any way in our happiness.

All have sinned and fall short of the glory of God (Rm 3:23), and therefore Peter's 'Repent!' is addressed to all of us. Repentance – the salvation word *par excellence* of our time. The Apocalypse contains seven letters to seven churches in Asia Minor (Rv 1:4). Each one of these letters ends with a warning: 'If anyone has ears to hear, let him listen to what the Spirit is saying to the Churches.' A close reading shows that the word *metanòeson*, which means 'repent, convert', is prominently placed at the centre of each letter. He who has an ear to hear what the Spirit is

saying to the Church today knows he is saying the same
thing: 'Repent!'

On 9 October 1963, the night before the Vajont Dam
collapsed in Friuli, Italy, causing a terrible disaster, creaking noises were heard coming from the spot but no one
took any notice. Something similar is happening around
us today, if we are able to hear it. This world we have
built, mixing injustice and open rebellion to God's commandments, is creaking. There is a smell of burning in the
air. If John the Baptist were alive today, he would cry
to us, 'The axe is laid to the roots of the trees. Repent'
(Mt 3:10).

Even non-believers confusedly notice this obscure
threat hovering over us, but they react in a totally different
way: they build atomic shelters! Some nations are invest-
ing a great part of their budgets in these, as if this could
possibly solve the problem! We believers are also search-
ing for an atomic shelter, but ours, our 'Noah's ark', is our
repentance for our sins. In fact, nothing or no one can
frighten him whose heart is fixed in God, the steady rock.
He sings with the psalmist:

> God is our shelter, our strength,
> ever ready to help in time of trouble,
> so we shall not be afraid when the earth gives way,
> when mountains tumble into the depths of the sea.
> (Ps 46:1–2)

To this unbridled world threatening me with destruction, I feel that I can repeat in faith those well-known
words, 'Thou hast not half the power to do me harm – as I
have to be hurt' (Shakespeare). Because 'There is nothing
I cannot master with the help of the One who gives me

strength' (Ph 4:13). He said, 'Be brave; I have conquered the world' (Jn 16:33). And I believe him!

* * *

And now we have come to another wonderful verse in Peter's sermon, 'But God raised him up.' By resurrecting Jesus from the dead, God transformed our greatest sin into his greatest mercy. By killing Jesus we have killed our sins which he had taken on to himself. Only if the word 'repentance' has reached the bottom of our hearts shall we be able to savour now the floods of light and love enclosed in this joyful Easter message. Whoever has been able to say in all sincerity, 'I killed Jesus of Nazareth,' knows what it means to be 'born anew to a living hope through resurrection of Jesus Christ from the dead' (1 P 1:3). It is like someone being convinced he has killed another person and who flees in desperation, believing there is no escape in this world for him, when, unexpectedly, he hears that the person managed to survive and has forgiven him and even wants to be friends with him.

Sin itself holds no fear for us because we no longer bear it by ourselves. He was 'raised to life to justify us' (Rm 4:25), that is, so that he could take our sins and, in exchange, grant us his justice. A repentant man has descended to Hell with Jesus, he has been 'baptised in his death' (Rm 6:3), and now it's as if Jesus were dragging him together with himself out of the tomb and into a new life. 'But God loved us with so much love that he was generous with his mercy: when we were dead through our sins, he brought us to life with Christ' (Ep 2:4–5).

Perhaps you think this joyful message is not for you because your veil hasn't been torn and your eyes haven't overflowed with tears of repentance. Don't be sad and don't despair; this is God's gift and he can give it to you from one minute to the next, or gradually, perhaps when you least expect it. Just persevere untiringly in imploring him and desiring it, just as I do. If you ardently long for repentance, you have already repented! Let yourself be born again to 'a living hope' and begin to live your new life.

Look at all the people around you and say to yourself, 'These are my brothers, they are all my brothers!' When you leave here, look with new eyes at the people you meet, the members of your family, of your community, those at work, and say to yourself, 'These are my brothers, they are all my brothers!' 'They were all born there,' that is, in the heart of Jesus pierced for our sins!

Now it is the risen Christ himself who is talking to us. The words are full of faith and enthusiasm and were used at a liturgical service like this one, by a bishop of one of the seven Churches of Asia Minor, at the beginning of the Church:

I destroyed death, and triumphed over the enemy,
I carried man to the high heavens:
Come, then, come all mankind
immersed in sin.
Receive the remission of your sin:
For I am your resurrection and the Passover of your
    salvation,
I am the lamb immolated for you,
I am your ransom,
your life,
your resurrection,
your light,
your salvation,
your king.
I will show you the Father.
(Melito of Sardis, *On Easter,* 102–3)

4

Baptised in his death

WHAT IS THE significance of the rite we are celebrating? Why are we gathered here this evening? The most obvious answer is to celebrate the Lord's death! But that's not enough. St Augustine says that 'Easter is not simply an anniversary but a mystery' (*sacramentum*). Now, to celebrate a mystery, we are not satisfied with recalling the past event on the day it took place, but we recall it so as to participate in it' (St Augustine, *Epistle*, 55, 1:2). Therefore, the liturgy of the Easter triduum is not significant only from a purely historical or moral aspect (a commemoration of the events and an exhortation to imitate them), it also has a mystic significance. Something must happen. We cannot remain on the outside, like simple spectators or listeners; we must go inside, as it were, become 'actors', and parties to the case.

And so we are here this evening to 'act' and not simply to 'recall'. And what we must do is be baptised into Christ's death! Let us listen to St Paul: 'You have been taught that when we were baptised in Christ Jesus we were baptised in his death; in other words, when we were baptised we went into the tomb with him and joined him in death, so that as Christ was raised from the dead by the Father's glory, we too might live a new life' (Rm 6:3–4).

But, we might wonder, didn't all this take place on the day of our baptism? What have we still got to do that hasn't been done? The answer is both yes and no. All this has already taken place and has yet to take place. If to be baptised means to be 'buried with Christ in death', then our baptism is not yet concluded. In the rite of baptism, a shorter formula has always existed for babies baptised *in articulo mortis*, that is, in danger of death. When the danger has passed, these babies must be taken to church again so as to complete the sacrament. We Christians today have been nearly all baptised *in articulo mortis*. We were baptised in a hurry during our first days of life for fear that death would overtake us. It is the usual procedure, and actually goes back to the beginnings of the apostolic era. However, once we become adults, we too should complete rites but with something essential which determines the efficacy of the Sacrament, even if not its validity. What is this something? Jesus says, 'Go out to the whole world; proclaim the Good News to all creation. He who believes and is baptised will be saved' (Mk 16:15–16).

He who believes and is baptised; two things always appear together in the New Testament whenever the beginning of salvation is mentioned, and they are faith and baptism (Jn 1:12; Acts 16:30–33; Ga 3:26–27). Baptism is 'the divine seal on the faith of the believer' (St Basil).

However, it is a question of a special type of faith that involves the whole person, a conversion-faith, 'Repent, and believe the Good News' (Mk 1:15), or also of a repentance-faith, 'You must repent . . . and every one of you must be baptised in the name of Jesus Christ' (Acts 2:38).

In the early Church Christians arrived at baptism through a process of conversion involving the whole of

[33]

life. The symbols used in the rite were visible signs of the break with the old life and the start of a new one. The catechumen stripped himself and went into the water; for an instant he was without light, breathless, dead to the world as if he were buried. Then he re-emerged into the light of the world. But, for him, the light and the world were no longer the same; it was a new light and a new world. He was 'born again by water and the Spirit'.

Is it possible to repeat this strong experience in the present situation? Yes, it is, and, actually, it is God's will that this should take place at least once in every Christian's life. One day Jesus said, 'I have come to bring fire to the earth, and how I wish that it were blazing already! There is a baptism I must still receive, and how great is my distress till it is over' (Lk 12:49–50). Jesus was thinking of his own death when he said these words, as the image of baptism used elsewhere in this way indicates (Mk 10:38). By his death on the cross, it is as if Jesus cast fire upon the earth and in his pierced side inaugurated a baptistry. This will remain open to the end of time because Jesus 'put to death in the flesh is alive in the Spirit' (1 P 3:18). In fact, that 'fire' is the Spirit which 'will be with us for ever' (Jn 14:16). Thanks to this living Spirit, all that concerns Jesus is relevant here and now for us.

To be baptised in Christ's death means to enter the burning bush; it means an agony. An agony, because it involves purification, aridity, crosses. But it is a prelude to birth and not to death; it is the pain of birth. To be baptised into Christ's death means to enter into his heart and to participate in God's drama of love and pain. To be baptised into his death is something that has to be lived and cannot be described. Whoever experiences it emerges a new person, ready to serve the Kingdom in a new way.

* * *

Let us now give concrete form to all this. What does it mean to be baptised into the death of Christ? Paul goes on to say, 'When he died, he died, once for all, to sin, so his life now is life with God; and in that way you too must consider yourselves to be dead to sin but alive for God in Christ Jesus' (Rm 6:10–11).

To be baptised into Christ's death means therefore to die to sin and live for God! To die to sin or 'cease from sin' (1 P 4:1) precisely implies making a firm decision, which as far as we are concerned is irrevocable, never to commit wilful sin again, especially 'that sin' to which we are still a little secretly attached.

The aim and ultimate goal is not death but life; rather, it is a new life, resurrection, joy, the inexpressible experience of the Father's love. But all of this is God's part; it is like the new robe he keeps ready for those who emerge from the waters of baptism. We must allow God to do his part, knowing that his faithfulness is as firm as heaven itself. We must do our part, which is to die to sin; we must leave behind the state of connivance with sin or even tacit solidarity with it. We must leave Babylon behind. Babylon, explains St Augustine in *The City of God*, is the city built on self-love which reaches the point of contempt for God; it is Satan's city. Babylon is therefore the lie, it is living for self, for self-glory. It is to this spiritual Babylon that God alludes when he says, 'Come out, my people, away from her, so that you do not share in her crimes and have the same plagues to bear' (Rv 18:4). It is not a question of really leaving the city or solidarity with mankind behind. It is a question of leaving a moral situation, not a place. It is not an escape from the world, but an escape from sin.

To die to sin means to enter into God's judgement. God looks on this world and judges it. His judgement is the only precise demarcation line between good and evil, between light and darkness. His judgement does not change with the times. To convert means to break through the wall of the lie and go over to the side of truth, and that is, to God's side. The decision is made when a man says to God with the psalmist, 'For I am well aware of my faults . . . You are just when you pass sentence on me, blameless when you give judgement' (Ps 51:3, 4). In other words, he is saying, 'I accept your judgement on me. O God, it is right and holy, it is love and salvation for me.'

With the coming of Christ, God's 'judgement' became visible, as if it had materialised and become historicised – it is Christ's cross! Before dying, and in allusion to his death on the cross, he said, 'Now sentence is being passed on this world; now the prince of this world is to be over-thrown' (Jn 12:31).

The cross is God's powerful 'no' to sin. It has been planted as the tree of life in the middle of the street of the city (Rv 22:2), in the middle of the Church and the world, and no one will ever be able to uproot it again, or substi-tute it with other principles. Today, as in St Paul's time, the 'Greeks', that is, scholars, philosophers and theologians, are still seeking wisdom; the 'Jews', that is, the devout and the faithful, are still demanding signs, accomplishment, efficiency and results; but the Church continues to preach Christ crucified, the power of God and the wisdom of God (1 Co 1:22–23).

* * *

On 11 November 1215, Pope Innocent III opened the Fourth Lateran Council with a memorable discourse. He started with the words Jesus used when he sat down to eat before his death, 'I have longed to eat this passover with you' (Lk 22:15). Passover, explained the pope, signifies a passing. And Jesus wants to make a triple passing with us here today: a corporal passing, a spiritual passing and an eternal passing. The corporal passing was, for the pope, the passing towards Jerusalem to reconquer the Holy Sepulchre; the spiritual passing was that from vice to virtue, from sin to grace, and therefore the moral renewal of the Church; the eternal passing was death, the final passing from this world to the Father. In this discourse, the pope insisted above all on the spiritual passing – the moral reform of the Church and especially of the clergy – a theme close to his heart. In fact, old as he was, he said he wished to go through the whole Church, like the man clothed in linen, with a writing case at his side, of whom Ezekiel speaks (Ezk 9:1 ff), to mark the penitential *tau* on the foreheads of those who, like him, sigh and groan over all the abominations that are committed in it and in the world.

He was never able to realise this dream as he died a few months later, thus making the third passing into the heavenly Jerusalem. But, as tradition tells us, in the Lateran Basilica where Innocent III held his discourse, hidden by the crowd and probably unrecognised by anyone, was a poor mendicant, named Francis of Assisi! At any rate, it is certain that he made the pope's ardent wish his own. From that day on his preaching on penance and conversion intensified and he began to mark the *tau* sign on the foreheads of those who were sincerely converted to Christ. The *tau*, the prophetic sign of Christ's cross, became his seal. He signed his letters with it, he drew it on the friars' cells, to the point that, after his death, St Bonaventure said, 'He was given the mission from heaven to call men to sigh and groan and shave their heads and put on sackcloth and ashes and to imprint the sign of the *tau*, the penitential cross, on the foreheads of all those that sigh and groan' (*Major Life*, 2). This was Francis's chosen 'crusade' – to sign the cross, not on clothes and arms to fight the 'infidels', but to imprint it in his own heart and in his brethren's hearts, to eliminate infidelity in God's people. He received this mission 'from heaven', St Bonaventure wrote, but now we know that he received it also from the Church, and specifically from the pope. He wanted to be a humble instrument in the service of the Church and her hierarchy, to accomplish the renewal started by the council of his day. This year, as we celebrate the eighth centenary of the birth of Francis of Assisi, we implore God to give his Church men like him to implement the renewal started by the ecumenical council of our day, Vatican II.

5

Crucified through weakness, Christ lives through the power of God

THROUGHOUT THE BIBLE, together with the revelation of God's power, there exists a secret revelation which could be called the revelation of God's weakness. God's weakness is linked with what Holy Scripture often calls 'the tender mercy of our God' (Jr 31:30; Lk 1:78). This, as it were, makes him impotent before sinful and wayward man. The people 'turn away', 'they are bent on turning away'. And in answer, God says, 'How could I part with you? Israel, how could I give you up? . . . My heart recoils from it, my whole being trembles at the thought' (Ho 11:8). Almost as if he were asking to be excused for this weakness, God says, 'Does a woman forget her baby at the breast, or fail to cherish the son of her womb?' (Is 49:15). In actual fact, this love is, above all, a mother's love. It springs from her innermost self where her child is formed and grips her whole being, body and soul. Her child is part of herself and she will never be able to cut it away without deeply wounding her very being.

God's weakness is therefore caused by his love for man. What a sorrow it is to impotently stand by while a loved one destroys himself with his own hands! The parents of drug addicts know what it is like, as day after day they are forced to witness the slow destruction of a son or daughter and often cannot even mention the real cause of the illness for fear of causing an irremediable breach. But couldn't God who is all powerful prevent this? He certainly could, but in so doing he would also be destroying man's freedom, and would thus be destroying man! So he can only admonish, beseech and warn us, which he constantly does through the prophets.

However, the measure of God's suffering was hidden from us until it took on a visible form in Christ's passion. Christ's passion is simply the historic and visible manifestation of the Father's suffering for man. It is the supreme manifestation of God's weakness. St Paul says that Christ was 'crucified through weakness' (2 Co 13:4). Man has prevailed over God, sin is victorious and triumphantly rises up before Christ's cross. The light is covered by the dark. But only for an instant; Christ was crucified through weakness but, the apostle continues, 'He lives now through the power of God'. He lives! He lives! And he now repeats to his Church, 'I was dead and now I am to live for ever and ever, and I hold the keys of death and of the underworld' (Rv 1:18). Truly, 'God's weakness is stronger than human strength' (1 Co 1:25). The cross has become God's power, God's wisdom, God's victory. God has prevailed, not by denying his weakness, but rather by pushing it to the extreme. He refused to fight the enemy with the same weapon: 'He was insulted and did not retaliate with insults' (1 P 2:23). His response to man's will to annihilate him was not to destroy man in return but to save him, 'As I live,' he says, 'I take pleasure, not in the death of a wicked man, but in the turning back of a wicked man who changes his ways to win life' (Ez 33:11). A Church prayer tells us that God manifests his omnipotence in mercy and forgiveness (*parcendo et miserando*). In response to the cry of 'Crucify him!' he cried out, 'Father, forgive them!' (Lk 23:34).

No words can compare with these three words, 'Father, forgive them!' They contain all God's power and holiness; they are indomitable words which no crime or offence can overcome, for they were uttered just when evil was at its most powerful peak, which it can never again reach. 'Death is swallowed up in victory. Death, where is your victory? Death, where is your sting?' (1 Co 15:54–55). Those words, 'Father forgive them' are like sacramental words. They express the meaning and purpose of the passion – which is the reconciliation of the world with God – and, in expressing it, they cause it. *Significando causant*, as we used to say in our theology of the sacraments.

This reconciliation began immediately at the cross with Christ's crucifiers. I am convinced that Christ's crucifiers were saved and that we shall meet them in heaven. They will bear witness for eternity to the extent of the Lord's goodness. Jesus prayed for them with all his power, 'Father, forgive them!' and the Father who had always heard his Son's prayer in life (Jn 11:42) cannot but have heard this prayer of his Son at the moment of death. After the crucifiers come the good thief and then the centurion (Mk 15:39) and then the crowd that converted on the day of Pentecost. This procession has gone on swelling and swelling and embraces us who are here this evening to celebrate Christ's death. In the book of Isaiah, God says of the suffering servant, 'By his sufferings shall my servant justify many . . . for surrendering himself to death and letting himself be taken for a sinner, while he was bearing the faults of many and praying all the time for sinners' (Is 53:11, 12). Because he took their faults upon himself, saying, 'Father, forgive them!' he justified many!

We have a distorted view of the redemption, and this

creates problems of faith for us. We think of it as a sort of bargain: Jesus, the mediator between God and man, pays the Father the price of our ransom with his blood and the Father is 'satisfied' and forgives men their sins. But this is a very human view, inexact or at least partially so. Even humanly speaking it is unbelievable – a father who needs his son's blood to be placated! The truth is that the Son's suffering comes first and foremost (it is spontaneous and free!), and this is so precious in the Father's eyes that he, in return, makes the greatest gift possible to the Son, giving him many brothers, making him 'the eldest among many brothers' (Rm 8:29). 'Ask', he told him, 'and I will give you the nations for your heritage, and the ends of the earth for your domain' (Ps 2:8).

Therefore, it is not so much the Son paying a debt to the Father as the Father paying a debt to the Son for having restored to him 'all those who had gone astray'. And he paid it as only God could, in an infinite measure, for none of us could possibly imagine the glory and joy the Father gave Christ in his resurrection.

* * *

Commenting on the 'Our Father', a Christian poet makes God say these words that ring even truer if we apply them to the prayer of Jesus on the cross:

As the spreading wake of a ship is lost on the horizon;
But it starts at a point, and this point moves towards
    me.
The ship is my Son carrying all the sins of the world.
And the point is the words, *Father, forgive them!*
He well knew what he was doing that day, my Son who
    loves them,

[42]

When he placed this barrier between them and me,
    Father, forgive them!
Just these three words.
Like a man who had placed a mantle on his shoulders
He stood before me.
He had placed on his shoulders
the mantle of the sins of the world.
And now, behind that mantle, the sinner hides from
    me.
They have gathered as if in fear; and who can blame
    them?
Like frightened sparrows they have gathered behind
    the strong one.
And they offer me this point.
And thus they pierce the wind of my anger and
    triumph over the powerful tempests of my
    justice.
And the breeze of my anger makes no impression on
    this angular host of slippery wings.
For this angle: *Father, forgive them!* is all that they
    present.
And only from this angle can I receive them.
         (Charles Péguy, *The Mystery of the Holy Innocents*)

Maybe the wake of that 'ship' is passing by close to us right now, this Easter. Let us not remain on the outside; let us fly into the arms of the God of mercy; let us take shelter against that point. Let us be part of the joyful procession of those ransomed by the Lamb. It is the Church that is now entreating us in the words of the apostle Paul, 'Be reconciled to God!' (2 Co 5:20). God suffered for you, for you individually, and he would be ready to do so again if it were necessary for your salvation. Why do you wish to lose yourself? Why mortify your God by saying that all of this doesn't interest you? God is of no interest to you, but you are of interest to God! To the point of dying for you. Have compassion for your God, do not be cruel with him and with yourself. Like the prodigal son, prepare in your heart what you want to say to him and move towards him who is waiting for you.

* * *

We know why many don't want to be reconciled with God. People say there is too much innocent suffering in the world, too much unjust suffering. Reconciliation with God would mean reconciliation with injustice, acceptance of the pain of the innocent, and we can't accept that! You can't believe in a God who allows the innocent to suffer (Albert Camus); the suffering of the innocent is 'the rock of atheism' (Georg Büchner).

This is a terrible deception! Those innocent ones are now singing the Lamb's hymn of victory 'You are worthy to take the scroll and to break the seals of it, because you were sacrificed and with your blood you bought men for God of every race, language, people and nation' (Rv 5:9). They follow the Lamb's 'wake' while we, instead, stand on that unhappy 'rock'. It is true that there is much innocent suffering in the world, far more than we can possibly imagine, but this does not usually keep those that suffer far from God (nothing brings us closer to him), but rather those that write essays on or discuss, in comfort, the suffering of the innocent. These suffering innocents (beginning with the thousands of babies killed in their mother's wombs) are one 'mass' with God's innocent Son. Baptised or not, they are part of that greater and hidden Church which began with Abel the just, and which embraces all those persecuted and the victims of sin in the world: the *Ecclesia ab Abel.* Their suffering is their baptism of blood.

[44]

Like the Holy Innocents, celebrated by the liturgy immediately after Christmas, they confess Christ not with words but with their deaths. They are the salt of the earth. Just as Christ's death was mankind's greatest sin and yet it saved humanity, the suffering of the numerous victims of hunger, injustice and violence is the greatest sin of mankind today and yet it contributes to its salvation. If we haven't yet gone under, we owe it to them too, perhaps, and how could we say it was all useless and wasted? We think it is wasted suffering because we no longer really believe in the eternal reward of the just, in God's faithfulness. It is not so much the impossibility of explaining suffering that causes the loss of faith as the loss of faith that makes it impossible to explain suffering.

* * *

On a day like today, God says to the pastors of his people, Forgive as I forgive; I forgive in my heart, I am deeply moved to pity by the misery of my people. And neither must you just utter the cold formula of forgiveness with your lips. I need your hearts and not just your lips to communicate my mercy and compassion. Clothe yourselves with 'warm and tender compassion'. There is no sin too great or too dreadful. Repeat to yourself and to the brother before you, 'Yes, but God's compassion is far, far greater.' You must be like the father in the parable who goes to meet his prodigal son and throws his arms around his neck. May the world not feel so much the judgement of the Church as the mercy and compassion of the Church. Do not give penances that the sinner is not yet ready for; do penance yourselves for him and you will be like my Son. I love these sons who have gone astray and, in due course, I shall give them time to make amends for their sins. Love my people whom I love!

[45]

To those suffering in body or soul, the old, the sick, who feel useless and maybe envy those who are healthy around them, I say in all humility and respect: Look how God behaved! There was a time in creation when God worked with power and joy; he spoke and all was done; he commanded and all existed. But when he wanted to do something greater still, he stopped working and started to suffer; he invented his own annihilation and so redeemed us. Because in God too, and not only in man, 'power is at its best in weakness' (2 Co 12:9). You are cheek to cheek with Christ on the cross. If your suffering is caused by others, say with Jesus, 'Father, forgive them!' and the Father will give you too the 'reward' of that brother for eternal life.

To all, I repeat the great news of today: Christ was crucified through weakness, but lives through the power of God!

6

And at once there came out blood and water

ONE DAY, WHEN the temple of Jerusalem was destroyed and the people exiled to Babylon, the prophet Ezekiel had a vision. He saw before him the rebuilt temple and he saw water issuing from below the threshold of the temple, towards the east. He followed the line of water and he saw that it was getting deeper and deeper until it was ankle-deep, and then knee-deep, and then it was up to the loins and it became a river he could not pass through. Then he saw upon the bank of the river very many trees and he heard a voice saying, 'This water flows east down to the Arabah and to the sea; and flowing into the sea it makes its waters wholesome. Wherever the river flows, all living creatures teeming in it will live. Fish will be very plentiful, for wherever the water goes it brings health, and life teems wherever the river flows' (Ezk 47:8–9).

John the Evangelist saw this prophecy fulfilled in Christ's passion. He wrote, 'One of the soldiers pierced his side with a lance; and immediately there came out blood and water' (Jn 19:34). The Church sings these words in the liturgy at the beginning of every solemn Mass at Easter time as they now refer to Christ: *Vidi aquam egredientem de templo*, 'I saw water issuing from the temple.'

Jesus is the temple that man destroyed but that God rebuilt by raising him from the dead. He had said, 'Destroy this sanctuary, and in three days I will raise it up'; and the evangelist explains that 'He was speaking of the sanctuary that was his body' (Jn 2:19–21). On the cross, Christ's body became the new temple, the centre of the new worship, the final place of God's glory and presence among men. And from the right side of this new temple water flows. This, too, like the water seen by the prophet, started as a trickle but it grew and grew until it became a big river. In fact, from this trickle of water spiritually comes the water of all the baptistries in the Church. Pope Leo the Great had two Latin verses engraved on the Lateran Baptistry which reads: 'This is the wellspring that cleansed the whole world – having its source in Christ's wound' (*Fons hic est qui totum diluit orbem – sumens de Christi vulnere principium*). Truly, 'rivers of living water' have flowed from the heart of Christ on the cross!

* * *

But what does the water represent? One day (it was the last day of the Feast of Tabernacles) Jesus stood up and exclaimed, 'If any man is thirsty, let him come to me! Let the man come and drink who believes in me!' And the evangelist comments, 'He was speaking of the Spirit which those who believed in him were to receive' (Jn 7:37–39). The water, therefore, symbolises the Spirit. Referring to this episode, St John's first letter says, 'There are three witnesses, the Spirit, the water and the blood' (1 Jn 5:7–8). These three are not on the same level. The blood and water coming visibly from Christ's side were the signs, the sacraments; the Spirit was the invisible reality hidden in them and acting through them.

Before this moment the Spirit had not yet come into

the world; but now that Jesus had died for us, purifying us from our sins, the Spirit was moving over the face of the waters again as at the beginning of Creation (Gn 1:2). Having exclaimed, 'It is accomplished', Jesus 'gave up his spirit' (Jn 19:30), which means: He drew his last breath and died, but also: He gave forth his Spirit, the Holy Spirit! The evangelist means both. The last breath of Jesus became the first breath of the Church! This was the realisation of the work of redemption, its most precious fruit. Redemption was not just the remission of sins, it was also positively the gift of the new life of the Spirit. In fact, this was the aim of the whole thing, and the remission of sins itself is carried out in the Church today only through the Holy Spirit.

It is true that the Holy Spirit comes upon the Church at Pentecost in a solemn and public way. But in his gospel John wanted to show where the Spirit who came upon the apostles at Pentecost had come from; he wanted to show his source in the history of salvation. This source is the body of Christ glorified on the cross.

At the incarnation, and later on in another way at the baptism in the Jordan, the Father sent the fullness of the Holy Spirit upon his Son. This Spirit, as it were, gathered all his strength into the Saviour's humanity; he sanctified his human actions, inspired his words and guided all his choices. In him 'he learnt to live among men' (St Irenaeus). But during his earthly life he was hidden from the human eye like the fragrance in an alabaster vase (Jn 12: 3 ff). But now, the alabaster vase, the pure humanity of Christ, was broken during his passion and its fragrance has filled the whole house, that is, the Church.

'Wherever the river flows, all creatures will live', says the prophecy. This was also the effect of the stream that came from Christ's side. It brought back life to the world, so much so that the Church, wishing to briefly summarise her faith in the third person of the Trinity at Constantinople in 381, found nothing more essential to say about the Holy Spirit than that he gives life: 'I believe in the Holy Spirit who is Lord and giver of life.'

* * *

The news that the Spirit gives life is more necessary today than ever before, and it is something our present world is seeking. When St Paul arrived in Athens he saw that, in this city full of idolatry, the people were also looking for a new divinity to whom they had made an altar with the inscription, 'To the unknown God'. So the apostle started preaching and said, 'Men of Athens, . . . the God whom I proclaim is in fact the one you already worship without knowing it' (Acts 17:22–23). Then he spoke of the crucified and risen Christ. Something like this is happening today. Behind all the idolatry and materialism in our society, there is today a confused search for something new and different, something that does not end with us and gives an eternal meaning to our lives. There is a deep dissatisfaction that does not depend on the lack of things because often it is where there is too much that the dissatisfaction is greatest. And the mark of all this is sadness, a dreadful sadness for those who are not used to it. Even our children are being silently brought up to be sad.

A modern philosopher speaks of a 'nostalgia for the Totally Other' which is surfacing here and there in the world today. And the Church cries out to the men of today what the apostle said to the men of Athens. What is 'different', what you feel nostalgia for, does exist; it is God's Spirit! This Spirit is freedom, it is newness, beauty, it is joy. This Spirit is life. We struggle a lot today for higher standards of living. But in doing so we must not lose sight of the fact that there is also a different quality of life, without which all is vain. What's the use of living a *good* life, if we cannot expect an *everlasting* life?

* * *

How sweet therefore are the words Jesus is silently saying to us today from the cross:

> Oh, come to the water all you who are thirsty;
> though you have no money, come!
> Buy corn without money, and eat,
> and, at no cost, wine and milk. (Is 55:1)

The wound in my side is there for you, 'Look and see how good the Lord is.' Even those who have no money to pay – those without merit, those who feel unworthy and sinful, those who no longer have the strength to pray – come, take and eat. I ask only one thing in return: your thirst, your desire; that you do not feel satisfied and sufficient to yourselves. I am asking you for faith!

But now the temple of his body is no longer with us; where is Jesus inviting us? He is inviting us to come to the Church, to the sacraments of the Church! We can no longer see the temple of his human body, the body born of Mary and nailed to the cross, but his body, the Church, still exists. Again John the Evangelist, who in the gospel showed us the fulfilment of Ezekiel's prophecy on the cross, shows us its fulfilment in the Church in the Book of Revelation: 'Then the angel showed me the river of life, rising from the throne of God and of the Lamb and flowing crystal-clear down the middle of the city street. On either side of the river were the trees of life' (Rv 22:1–2). The water of life now flows through the holy city, the new Jerusalem which is the Church. Everyone who thirsts for the Spirit must turn to her. St Irenaeus, whose doctrine is directly based on that of a disciple of John's, warns us: 'God's gift is entrusted to the Church . . . because where the Church is, there also is God's Spirit, and where God's Spirit is, there also is the Church. They have no part in him who do not receive life at their Mother's breast and do not draw from the pure fountain coming from Christ's body but dig "cracked cisterns" and making holes in the earth, they drink dirty muddy water' (*Against the Heresies*, III, 24, 2).

On the Passover evening, Jesus came into the place where the disciples were and 'breathed on them and said, "Receive the Holy Spirit" ' (Jn 20:22). He did not just do this once and for all at his first Passover and then disappear form history, leaving the Church to make her own way with the means he had given her, until his return. That day, when he granted the apostles the power to forgive sins, he inaugurated in a solemn and visible way his new state as life-giving Spirit (1 Co 15:45). He lives now always 'breathing' on the Church; he has never ceased to do so for a moment. He is doing it now at this service. If he were to 'take away his Spirit', everything in the Church 'would die and return to dust', exactly as Scripture tells us happens with creation (Ps 104:29). 'Without the Holy Spirit, God is far away, Christ stays in the past, the Gospel is a dead letter, the Church simply an organisation, authority a matter of domination, mission a matter of propaganda, liturgy no more than an evocation, Christian living a slave morality. But with the Holy Spirit, the cosmos is resurrected and groans with the birth pangs of the kingdom, the risen Christ is there, the Gospel is the power of life, mission is a Pentecost, the liturgy is both memorial and anticipation, and human action is deified' (Ignatius of Latakieh).

Jesus, therefore, goes on 'breathing', but we believers have not always received and do not always receive his breath. Trusting as we do in our own efforts and human wisdom, we do not always give it importance. We are too taken with producing, doing, planning and discussing among ourselves. However, something now irresistibly urges us to pause and, with our hearts full of secret desire, to open ourselves again to the powerful breath of the risen Christ. A 'strong wind' has shaken the house again, since it was invoked on the Church 'as in a new Pentecost'.

'The hour will come – in fact it is here already', Jesus said one day, 'when the dead will hear the voice of the Son of God, and all those who hear it will live' (Jn 5:25). Yes, the hour is here. Today, in spite of the darkness looming here and there in the world, many Christians who were either dead or lukewarm are being revived through contact with the Spirit of Christ. They are born anew and discovering again the greatness of their baptism and are happy to work for evangelisation. In the midst of difficulties, they sing a new hymn of praise and glory to God who has worked wonderful graces in them. Magnificent flowers of holiness are blossoming here and there among the people of God in the heat of this divine breath.

* * *

In the 'pentecostal' revival, priests of the Church have a definite role and cannot remain on the outside as simple spectators for fear of the new. People who long for the 'Totally Other' often approach us priests. It is up to us to administer the 'life-giving Spirit' to the faithful. Let us not delude them; let us not offer empty and meaningless words about God to those who are seeking the living God. May the situation not be similar to that of Isaiah's time,

'The poor and the needy ask for water, and there is none' (Is 41:17).

That day, beneath the cross of Jesus, together with Mary, stood the youngest of the disciples, the disciple Jesus loved, the one who 'saw and gave testimony'. Today, too, Jesus is calling the young to come close to him at the foot of the cross. The Church has need of the young and pure of heart for the 'service of the Spirit'! It is a wonderful thing to leave all for Christ, to place oneself at his service in the religious and priestly life. It is a wonderful thing to form a human family, but it is even more wonderful to work to unite God's family. Therefore, if you hear his call today, do not harden your hearts. Just come! Do not be discouraged by our lukewarmness; you can become, and will become, better priests than us: new priests for a new Church!

Let us end with a prayer. Lord Jesus, breathe with power on your Church now gathered together all over the world to celebrate your passion; repeat your supreme words also over us: 'Receive the Holy Spirit!'

7

The righteousness of God has been manifested

A WRITER, WHO was also a believer and a poet, related in the third person of the greatest act of faith in his life. A man, he said (and we know he was talking about himself), had three children and one day all three fell ill. His wife was so worried that she withdrew into herself. She no longer even spoke. But he was different. He was a man and he wasn't afraid to talk. He had realised that the situation could no longer go on as it was. So he did something daring. He was rather pleased with himself over this, and it must be said that it really was a bold move. Just as one would pick up three children and place them in their mother's or their nurse's arms and she, delighted, would exclaim that there were too many of them to hold all at once, that they were too heavy, so he, taking his courage in both hands, had confidently placed, in prayer, his three sick children in the arms of her who holds all the suffering of the world. (The poet made a pilgrimage from Paris to Chartres to entrust his children to Our Lady.) 'Here,' he said, 'take them; I'm going to run away so that you can't give them back to me. You can see that I no longer want them!' How pleased he was with himself that he had had that stroke of genius! From that day on all went well, because it was the Blessed Virgin who was looking after them. It is strange that not all Christians behave in the same way. It is so simple really, but we never seem to think of simple things. We may as well admit at once that we are really rather silly (Charles Péguy).

I have started in this unusual way because today God's word is inviting us to do something equally daring. One day, explaining the significance of his death on the cross, Jesus said, 'The Son of Man must be lifted up as Moses lifted up the serpent in the desert, so that everyone who believes may have eternal life in him' (Jn 3:14). To believe is, therefore, the great task we have on Good Friday before Jesus crucified. He was 'raised up' on the cross and in a mysterious way he will be there to the end of time (even if he is risen) so that, contemplating him, mankind may believe.

What is it that we must believe? In his Letter to the Romans St Paul writes, 'God's justice that was made known through the Law and the Prophets has now been revealed outside the Law, since it is the same justice of God that comes through faith to everyone, Jew and pagan alike, who believes in Jesus Christ. Both Jew and pagan sinned and forfeited God's glory'. All have sinned – the only distinction being that some are aware of this, some still ignore it and others have forgotten it. But they are 'justified through the free gift of his grace by being redeemed in Christ Jesus who was appointed by God to sacrifice his life so as to win reconciliation through faith' (Rm 3:21–25).

This is what we must believe: that in Jesus Christ God offers us the chance to be justified through faith, made righteous, as it were, forgiven, saved, made new. This is what 'God's righteousness' means. God works his justice by showing mercy.

* * *

The way into this new creation is through faith. 'Repent, and believe the Good News,' was what Jesus said at the beginning of his ministry (Mk 1:15). Repent by believing! Enter the kingdom that has come to you! And now, after Easter, the apostles repeat the same thing, referring to the kingdom that has finally come, which is Jesus Christ crucified and risen.

The first basic conversion is faith. Faith is the gateway to salvation. If we were told that the gateway is innocence, that the gateway is a strict observance of the commandments, that it is this or that virtue, we could reply: It is not for me! I am not innocent, I lack that virtue. But we are told that the gateway is faith. Believe! This is not too great for you and nor is it too far from you; it is not on the other side of the world; on the contrary, 'The word, that is the faith we proclaim, is very near to you, it is on your lips and in your heart. If your lips confess that Jesus is Lord and if you believe in your heart that God raised him from the dead, then you will be saved!' (Rm 10:8–9).

There are various kinds of faith: faith as assent, faith as confidence and faith as obedience. Which of these is relevant to us now? We are concerned with a special kind of faith – faith as appropriation. The kind of faith that causes the bold stroke. 'What I can't obtain by myself', St Bernard said, 'I confidently appropriate to myself [literally, *usurpo*] from the pierced side of the Lord, for he is full of mercy. The mercy of God is, therefore, my merit. So, if "great is the mercy of the Lord" [cf. Ps 119:156], I too will abound in merit. And what about *my* justice? O Lord, I shall remember only *your* justice for it is also mine, because you are God's justice for me' (St Bernard, *On the Canticle*, 61). In fact, it is written that Jesus Christ was made 'our wisdom, and our virtue, and our holiness, and our freedom' (1 Co 1:30).

All these things are 'for us', they are ours, as it were. The obedience realised by Jesus on the cross is mine, his love for the Father is mine. His death itself is ours, it is our greatest treasure, a right to forgiveness that no sin of ours, however great, can cancel. It is as if we ourselves were dead, thus destroying within us 'the body of sin'. 'If one man died for all, then all have died' (2 Co 5:14).

It is true that we never think of the simple things! This is the simplest and clearest thing in the New Testament, but it is not easy to discover it. Usually, it is something we realise at the end of our spiritual journey and not at the beginning. All in all, it is a question of saying a simple 'yes' to God. God created man free so that he would freely accept life and grace; accept himself as being favoured by God who was only waiting for his 'yes'. Instead, man said 'no'. Now God offers man a second chance, like a new creation, a new beginning. He gives him Christ on the cross as his 'expiation' and asks him, 'Do you want to live by his grace, in him?' To believe means to answer, 'Yes, I will!', and so become a new creature 'created in Christ Jesus' (Ep 2:10).

* * *

This is the stroke of daring I mentioned, and it is amazing how few ever make it. St Cyril of Jerusalem, one of the Fathers of the Church, expressed the same idea in these terms: 'O the extraordinary goodness of God to man! Through years of struggle the righteous men of the Old Testament were pleasing to God. But what they obtained by a long and heroic service acceptable to God, is given to you by Jesus in the space of an hour. In fact, if you believe that Jesus Christ is Lord and that God raised him from the dead, you will be saved and led to heaven by Jesus himself who led the good thief there' (St Cyril of Jerusalem, *Cat-echesis*, 5, 10).

Another ancient author wrote: Imagine that an epic battle has taken place in a stadium. A brave man faced an opponent and with great effort and pain defeated him. You have not fought or struggled or been wounded, but if you admire the brave man from the terraces and rejoice with him over his victory, if you make a crown for him, provoke and rouse the audience for him, if you joyfully bow before the victor and kiss him; in short, if you get into such a frenzy of enthusiasm for him that you consider his victory yours, you will certainly have a part in the victor's reward. Moreover, imagine that the victor does not need his reward but more than anything else wants to see his supporter honoured, whose crowning would be reward enough for him, would not then the friend receive the crown without having fought or sweated? That is precisely what happens between us and Christ. Although we haven't struggled or fought (that is, although we are still without merit), yet by faith (as we are doing now in this service) we sing praise to Christ's struggle, and admire his victory and honour his reward and show him passionate and ineffable love; we appropriate to ourselves his wounds and his death (N. Cabasilas, *Life in Christ*, 1, 5; PG 150, 517).

The Book of Chronicles in the Old Testament tells us that just before a crucial battle for the survival of the people of Israel, God spoke these words to them through a prophet: 'You will not need to fight here. Take up your position, stand firm, and see what salvation the Lord has in store for you' (2 Ch 20:17). These words were completely fulfilled in the supreme battle in the history of salvation that was fought by Jesus against the prince of darkness.

Through faith we gather where we have not sown; we

did not endure the battle, yet we receive the reward. God offers this incredible chance to man in Christ. It is the only real 'bargain' in life because it lasts for ever, it makes us 'rich' for eternity. And is this not an unheard of stroke of luck?

* * *

St Paul says, 'Now the righteousness of God has been manifested.' 'Now' signifies first of all the *historical* moment in which Jesus died on the cross, and then it signifies the *sacramental* moment of our baptism when we were 'washed clean, and sanctified, and justified' (1 Co 6:11), and finally it signifies the *present* moment, the here and now of our lives – this moment that we are living. There is, therefore, something we must do now, at once; something that I myself, and not another in my place, must do so as not to leave everything in mid-air. It is true that justification by faith is the beginning of the supernatural life, but it is not a beginning quickly overtaken by other acts and duties. It is a beginning that is always relevant, that has always to be re-established and revived. God is always the one who freely loves first and justifies first; so man must always be the one to accept free justification by faith. An ancient homily attributed to St John Chrysostom tells us that 'life for every man begins with the moment of Christ's immolation for him. But Christ immolates himself for him at the moment in which he acknowledges this grace and becomes aware of the life this immolation has obtained for him' (in *Sources Chrétiennes*, 36, pp. 60 ff).

Now then, Christ has immolated himself for us. Everything will become true, relevant and operative for us if we gain awareness of what Christ has done for us, if we confirm it with our freedom, if we rejoice and give thanks for what took place on the cross. I can return home this evening with the most beautiful treasure. I can make such a wonderful move that I would be for ever congratulating myself for it. I can again place my sins in the arms of Christ on the cross like the man who placed his three sick children in the arms of the Holy Virgin and then fled without turning round for fear of having to take them back again. So, I can confidently stand before my heavenly Father and say to him, 'Father, look on me, I am your Jesus now! His justice is upon me; he has clothed me in the garments of salvation, he has wrapped me in the cloak of integrity' (Is 61:10). As Christ put on my iniquity, I have put on his sanctity. I have put on Christ (Ga 3:27). 'May Yahweh find joy in what he creates' (Ps 104:31). On the sixth day of the week of the new creation, that of Christ's death, God again looks on his creation and sees that it is again 'very good'.

What becomes of our boasting then? It is excluded, says Paul (Rm 3:27). There is no longer room for this dreadful worm that spoilt the first creation. All is grace! 'But man could never redeem himself or pay his ransom to God: it costs so much to redeem his life, it is beyond him' (Ps 49:7–8). It was God that ransomed us with the blood of Christ. Boasting, therefore, is excluded. And yet there is something mankind can boast about; it can boast of 'the cross of our Lord Jesus Christ' (Ga 6:14). 'If anyone wants to boast, let him boast about the Lord!' (1 Co 1:31). To be able to boast of God! What boast could be greater in heaven or on earth? Who could still be so foolish as to want to change such a divine object of boasting for one's own sake? Yes, we shall boast of you, Lord. Now and for ever!

8

The Lion of the tribe of Judah
has triumphed!

WE HAVE A reliable commentary on the reading of the passion we have just heard in this Good Friday service, a commentary written by John the Evangelist himself or, at any rate, by one of his closest disciples who knew what John taught. It is the fifth chapter of the Book of Revelation. Both texts refer to the same event on Calvary. The fourth gospel narrates it in a historical way and Revelation interprets and celebrates it in a prophetic and liturgical way.

In the fifth chapter of Revelation, the Easter event is presented in the form of a heavenly liturgy which, however, was inspired by the practical and earthly worship of the Christian community of the time. Anyone reading it then would have been able to distinguish the characteristics common to his own liturgical celebrations. The Easter liturgy that inspired John both in the gospel and in Revelation is that of the Quartodecimans who celebrated the Passover on the same day as the Jews, 14 Nisan, that is, on the anniversary of Christ's death and not of his resurrection; the day that places the Friday of Parasceve at the centre and sees even the resurrection from that standpoint. We know from history that the seven

Churches of Asia Minor, to which the Book of Revelation is addressed, all followed the Quartodeciman rite. St Polycarp, a disciple of John's, was bishop of one of these Churches, Smyrna, and towards the middle of the second century he came to Rome to discuss the question of the different dates of Easter with Pope Anicetus. The famous Quartodeciman Melito was bishop of another Church, Sardis.

Thus, the fifth chapter of Revelation is the best commentary on what we are celebrating. It refers to the same historical moment that we are reliving. It contains God's words, inspired words, addressed to us here and now. Let us hear them.

* * *

'I saw', it says, 'that in the right hand of the One sitting on the throne there was a scroll that had writing on back and front and was sealed with seven seals' (Rv 5:1). This book written on back and front signifies the history of salvation or, in practical terms, the Old Testament Scriptures that contain it. It was written on back and front, the Fathers of the Church explained, to indicate that it could be read according to the letter or according to the Spirit: in the literal sense, as it were, which is particular and temporary, or in the spiritual sense, which is universal and everlasting. However, in order to read it the scroll had to be unsealed, whereas it was sealed with seven seals. Before Christ, Scripture was like a score of an immense symphony on paper, whose powerful sound cannot be heard until we know its key. A minister of the queen of Ethiopia, returning from Jerusalem, was reading chapter 53 of Isaiah and he turned to Philip and asked him, 'Is the prophet referring to himself or someone else?' (Acts 8:34). (He was reading the passage which says, 'Like a sheep that is led to the slaugh-

terhouse, like a lamb that is dumb in front of its shearer.')
The key to the reading was still missing.

John's vision continued: 'Then I saw a powerful angel
who called with a loud voice, "Is there anyone worthy to
open the scroll and break the seals of it?" But there was no
one, in heaven or on the earth or under the earth, who
was able to open the scroll and read it. I wept bitterly.'
John (as is the very nature of the liturgy) takes us back in
spirit to the historical moment in which the event took
place or was about to take place. The prophet's weeping
evokes the weeping of the disciples at the moment of the
death of Jesus ('We hoped it was him . . .'), the weeping of
Mary Magdalen beside the empty tomb, the weeping of all
who were 'waiting for the redemption of Israel'.

'But one of the elders said to me,' continues the vision,
' "There is no need to cry: the Lion of the tribe of Judah,
the Root of David, has triumphed, and he will open the
scroll and the seven seals of it." ' *Enikesen! Vicit!* He has
triumphed! This is the news the seer was charged to make
re-echo in the Church, as the Church must make it re-
echo in the world for all time: the Lion of the tribe of
Judah has triumphed! (The 'Lion of the tribe of Judah' is
the Messiah, so called in the Book of Genesis by Jacob
when he was blessing his son Jude.) The long-awaited
event that gives a meaning to everything has taken place.
History can never go back. With one great effort history
has brought its centre of gravity forward and reached its
highest point. The fullness of time has been inaugurated.
'It is accomplished', *Consummatum est,* Jesus cried out
before he died (Jn 19:30).

That simple verb *enikesen,* he has triumphed, contains
the very principle that gives history a kind of absoluteness.
In fact, it gives eternal and universal value to an event that
took place at a given point in time and space. 'What once

took place cannot possibly not have taken place' (*Factum fieri infectum non potest*, as an ancient saying goes). No one knows better than the 'prince of this world' the tremendous force of this principle, which represents for history what the principle of non-contradiction represents for metaphysics. It is impossible to go back to the previous state of things. Nothing and no one in the world, no matter how hard they try, can change what happened, that is, that Jesus Christ died and rose again, that man is redeemed, the Church founded, the sacraments instituted, the kingdom of God established. 'The page that illuminates everything has been turned, like that big illustrated page of the missal. See it resplendent in red, the big page that separates the two Testaments. All doors open at the same time, all opposition is dissipated, all contradiction is resolved' (Paul Claudel). We too have listened during this service to what Isaiah 53 says of the lamb led to slaughter, but it was not necessary for us to wonder, like the queen's minister, who the prophet was referring to. We know who he was talking about because the scroll has been opened.

And how and when did all this happen? The vision continues, 'Then I saw, standing between the throne with its four animals and the circle of elders, a Lamb that seemed to have been sacrificed.' A slain Lamb, killed, and yet standing, that is, risen! Through his death and resurrection Christ fulfilled all this. He explained the Scriptures by fulfilling them; not in words but in actions. John clearly goes back to the scene of Calvary when, through his victorious death, Jesus 'fulfilled the Scriptures'. In Revelation Christ says, 'I was victorious myself and took my place with my Father on his throne' (Rv 3:21).

Here is how a poet pictured the scene told by the centurion who was present on Calvary.

> Never a death like this,
> and I've lost count . . .
> His struggle wasn't with death.
> Death was his servant,
> not his master.
> That wasn't a defeated man . . .
> On the cross,
> his conflict was with something far greater
> than bitter-tongued pharisees.
> No, he fought a different battle . . .
> Later he gave a great cry of victory.
> They were puzzled,
> But I know battles and fighters.
> I'd recognise a victor's shout,
> anywhere.
>
> (F. Topping, *An Impossible God*)

The victory was precisely his death accepted in total obedience to the Father and out of love for mankind. For John the Evangelist the resurrection only brought to light the hidden victory realised on the cross. Jesus is 'victor because he was victim' (*victor quia victima*) (St Augustine, *Confessions*, X, 43). There is no apparent change in the bread and water on the altar after consecration, whereas we know they are quite different from before. Similarly, Easter has not brought about any apparent change in the world, whereas, in fact, everything has changed and the world has become a 'new creation'.

* * *

Now why did John feel the need to remind the Church of

his time of these things? The question is relevant because I think it holds the very message this page of the New Testament has for us. It gives meaning and purpose to the liturgy we are celebrating.

One day John the Baptist sent two of his followers to ask Jesus, 'Are you the one who is to come, or have we got to wait for someone else?' (Mt 11:3). It seems that the forerunner had shared with his contemporaries, in part at least, the expectation of a glorious and triumphant Messiah, and was now puzzled by Christ's gentle and unassuming way which was much less brilliant than he had imagined. All told, it seems that he too experienced his crisis of faith, his 'scandal' about Jesus as Peter and the other apostles did for the same reason. We know the message Jesus sent back to John, 'Blessed is anyone who does not find me a cause of failing' (Mt 11:6). Something similar took place in the Christian community towards the end of the apostolic era. Peter's second letter tells us that here and there Christians were asking, 'What has happened to the promise of his coming? Since our Fathers died everything has gone on just as it has since the beginning of creation' (2 P 3:4).

The Book of Revelation was written for a Church in this situation which was faced with an awful doubt. Was it really true that he who was to come had come? Was it true that everything had changed? Or wasn't the opposite true, and everything was the same as before? Christ's disciples were being persecuted, pointed out, excluded from social advantages. The beast 'was allowed to make war against the saints and conquer them' (Rv 13:7). The ground was prepared for internal strife. Heresy appeared which tended to shift attention from practical life to speculation and gnosis in order to avoid the radical demands of the Christian calling and to allow them to come to terms with the pagan way of life.

To this Church tempted towards discouragement and 'tepidness' and which needed to rediscover its 'previous fervour', so as to face even martyrdom, if necessary, to this very Church the elder sent his powerful Easter cry like the blare of a trumpet: *Enikesen*, 'He has triumphed!' John wants to make all Christians visionaries, seers, like himself, people who are able to see what the world has become because of Christ's death.

In the colour spectrum there is an area close to the red that cannot be seen by the naked eye. These infra-red rays make it possible to grasp different aspects of our planet, and things which would otherwise be unknown to us. The picture that emerges is quite different from that of ordinary experience. The same thing happens where the invisible world is concerned. There is an aspect of reality, the aspect that does not pass with the passing of this world which cannot be seen with the 'naked' eye but only in the light of divine revelation. Man, even if very learned and wise, cannot even suspect it. It is the Easter picture of the world that emerges from the death and resurrection of Christ; it is the world seen as God himself sees it. It does not just show another aspect of reality but shows everything in a new light, even earthly things. John had this picture, was imbued with it, and now he transmits it with all his prophetic power to the Church. He never tires of repeating, 'If anyone has ears to hear, let him listen to what the Spirit is saying to the churches' (Rv 2:7).

* * *

The question and temptation the forerunner felt for a moment ('Are you the one who is to come?'), and that felt by Christians of the second generation ('What has happened to this promise of his coming?') are present also today and are as relevant as ever. It all seems to continue just as it was ever since the creation of the world. Today too the beast is 'allowed to make war against the saints and conquer them'. Those who believe and, in a different way, all those who are upright of heart and men of good will, are often losers in all fields. The age-old adversary creeps into things to weaken the resistance of those who love truth and justice most and are most sensitive to suffering and evil in the world. And while on Good Friday the Church proclaims to the world that this is the day of the great redemption, the adversary torments these souls with the cry: 'This is the day of the great lie, this is the day of the great lie! Look around you, what is there that looks redeemed in the world?'

Today too the accuser falls as if struck by lightning (Rv 12:10; Lk 10:18) each time we pronounce the prophet's words with faith, *Vicit leo de tribu Juda*, 'the Lion of the tribe of Judah has triumphed' and has opened the scroll. All is redeemed because even suffering and death itself have been redeemed. The more the person repeating these words suffers, is defeated and weak, humanly speaking, the higher his cry reaches, shaking the very foundations of the powers of darkness, for thus is his faith purified like silver in the melting pot and above all, because he thus most resembles the Lamb who became a *victor* by accepting to be a *victim*. Before the tomb of her dead brother, Jesus said to Martha, 'Have I not told you that if you believe you will see the glory of God?' (Jn 11:40). He repeats the same words to each one of us when, humanly speaking, there seems to be no solution: 'Have I not told you that if you believe you will see the glory of God?'

Here on earth we do not just have faith in victory, we also have victory in faith. By faith we are already victors

[69]

experiencing something of eternal life. He who believes already sits 'with Jesus on his throne' and tastes 'the hidden manna' (Rv 2:17; 3:21). John powerfully reminds us of this: 'This is the victory over the world – our faith' (1 Jn 5:4).

There was a time when it was easier to proclaim the victory of the cross. 'The cross, once a sign of outrage, now shines on the crowns of kings,' some of the Fathers of the Church used to say when the persecution ended (St Augustine, *On the Psalm*, 75, 10). Didn't Constantine perhaps in his well-known vision of the cross hear the promise, 'By this sign you will have victory', *In hoc signo vinces*? However, it is no longer so, and especially in nations of the oldest Christian tradition. The cross is being removed from one place after another. Now, therefore, more than ever it is time to proclaim that the Lion of the tribe of Judah has triumphed. John himself received the message when he was 'on the island of Patmos for having preached God's word and witnessed for Jesus' (Rv 1:9), that is, when he was in exile. 'Blessed is he who does not find me a cause of failing,' Jesus continues to say.

When we are overwhelmed by situations that are too big for us, or when God's plan for our life, or for the lives of those dear to us, or for the entire Church, appears to be a scroll sealed with seven seals and we have to bear it without comprehending it, or when we see the poor and weak dying in the midst of indifference, then is the time for us to kneel and cry out with all our faith, 'The Lion of the tribe of Judah has triumphed and he will open the scroll and the seven seals of it!' In him all those defeated and all the victims of the world have been given the hope of becoming victors.

* * *

The Lion of the tribe of Judah has triumphed!

It is written that as soon as the Lamb took the scroll from the hand of him who was seated on the throne, a powerful chorus echoing all over heaven and earth was heard singing, 'You are worthy to take the scroll and break the seals of it, because you were sacrificed.' And it is also written that in the end, all 'prostrated themselves to worship'. And that is what we shall do in a few minutes when we prostrate ourselves in worship before the cross, thus prolonging on earth the divine liturgy of heaven. 'I wept bitterly,' says the prophet of himself at the beginning of the vision, and the Church too weeps today. She weeps for the death of her Spouse on the cross, she weeps amid the tribulations of the world, she weeps for the defection and hardness of heart of many of her children, she weeps for her own unfaithfulness. It is to this Church of contrite and humble heart, gathered around the Lamb with her pastor and pontif, that these words full of joy and hope are addressed, 'There is no need to cry', *enikesen*, the Lion of the tribe of Judah, the Root of David, has triumphed. He has triumphed!

9

He was pierced through for our faults

'WHEN WE WERE baptised in Christ Jesus', wrote St Paul, 'we were baptised in his death' (Rm 6:3). The immersion in the water at the moment of baptism was therefore a visible exterior sign of another 'bath' and another 'burial', that in the death of Christ. However, what happened both ritually and symbolically at the beginning must be realised in faith, put into practice at least once in our lifetime, if it is not to remain just a symbol. We must take a wholesome bath in Christ's passion, we must go down into it in spirit and feel upon us all the cold and bitterness it contains so as to emerge renewed and fortified.

It is written that there was a miraculous pool in Jerusalem and the first to go down into it when the water moved was cured. We must go down into the pool, or rather, into the ocean of Christ's passion. Because such is the suffering of the God-man, a boundless ocean, shoreless and bottomless.

There exists a passion of Christ's soul which is the soul of the passion or, as it were, that which gives it universal and transcendent value. Many have suffered the physical pain that Jesus suffered, if not greater. From a mere physical point of view, all the pain suffered by men throughout the centuries put together would form a greater mass of suffering than that which Jesus took on himself, whereas all the torment and anguish of men put together will never, even remotely, be near the passion of the Redeemer's soul.

St Paul expresses this passion when he says, 'For our sake God made the sinless one into sin, so that in him we might become the goodness of God' (2 Co 5:21). God's own Son, the innocent one, the holy one, has become 'sin'. Jesus is a man made sin.

In Gethsemane, Jesus prayed, 'Let this cup pass me by!' (Mt 26:39). In the Bible the cup image almost always evokes the idea of God's anger against sin (Rv 14:10). Isaiah calls it the 'cup of stupor' (Is 51:22). St Paul says, 'The anger of God is being revealed from heaven against all impiety' (Rm 1:18). It is a sort of universal principle. Where there is sin, there God's anger and his tremendous 'no' cannot but appear. Otherwise, God himself would be compromising with sin, the distinction between good and evil would disappear, and the entire universe would collapse. God's anger is not like man's; it is another name to indicate God's holiness.

Now Jesus in his passion is ungodliness, all the ungodliness of the world. And therefore God's anger is against him. 'In that body God condemned sin' (Rm 8:3).

A correct understanding of Christ's passion is hindered by a too legalistic view of things. We see humankind and its sins on the one hand, and on the other, Jesus suffering and expiating those sins, remaining, however, at a distance, whereas the relationship between Jesus and sin is not indirect and only legalistic, but close and real. In other words, the sins were on him, mysteriously on him, because he had freely 'taken' them. It is written, 'He was bearing our faults in his own body' (1 P 2:24). In some way, he felt he was the sin of the world and in this consisted the passion of his spirit.

* * *

For once we must give sin a name and a concrete form so that it does not just remain an abstract idea or something irrelevant for us as it is for the world. Jesus took on himself all human pride, all open or silent rebellion against God, all lustfulness (which is, and will remain, sin, even if we were all to uphold the contrary), all forms of hypocrisy, violence and injustice, the exploitation of the poor and weak, all lies and the dreadful sin of hatred.

In Christ's passion, the words of Isaiah we heard in the first reading find their realisation, 'He was pierced through for our faults, . . . On him lies a punishment that brings us peace' (Is 53:5). He is the 'suffering servant' who prays in the psalms and says to the Father, 'Weighted down by your anger, drowned beneath your waves . . . your anger overwhelmed me, you destroyed me with your terrors' (Ps 88: 7, 16).

What would happen if the physical universe with all its galaxies rested on one point only, like an immense inverted pyramid? What pressure would that point have to bear? Well, the whole moral universe of sin, no less immense than the physical one, weighed on the God-man in the passion. It is written that the Lord 'burdened him with the sins of all of us' (Is 53:6); he is the Lamb of God who 'carried' the sin of the world, (Jn 1:29). The real cross Jesus carried on his shoulders all the way to Calvary and to which he was finally nailed was sin!

Because Jesus took on sin, God is far away. The infinite attraction that existed between the Father and the Son is now crossed by a repulsion just as infinite. In the Alps in summer, when a mass of cold air from the north clashes with hot air from the south, frightful storms break out disturbing the atmosphere; dark clouds move around, the wind whistles, lightning rends the sky from one end to the other and the thunder makes the mountains tremble. Something similar took place in the Redeemer's soul where the extreme evil of sin clashed with the supreme holiness of God disturbing it to the point that it caused him to sweat blood and forced the cry from him, 'My soul is sorrowful to the point of death. Wait here, and keep awake' (Mk 14:34).

Speaking of his fellow Jews, St Paul says that because of their refusal of the Gospel he feels such great sorrow for them that he could wish himself to be *anàtema*, cut off from Christ, for the sake of his brothers (Rm 9:3). What the apostle perceived to be the utmost privation without having to actually experience it, Jesus really experienced to the very end on the cross. He became *anàtema*, cut off from God for the sake of his brothers. In fact, 'Christ redeemed us from the curse of the Law by being cursed for our sake, since scripture says: Cursed be everyone who is hanged on a tree' (Ga 3:13). Being cursed, *katàra*, is almost the same as being *anàtema*; it indicates separation from God and men, a sort of excommunication.

The experience of the silence of God which modern man feels so acutely can help us understand something of Christ's passion so long as we keep in mind that the significance of God's silence for modern man is not the same as for biblical man. The pain caused by God's silence is measured by the intensity with which his name is invoked. The greater the trust placed in God and the more ardent the prayer, the more painful is God's silence. We can therefore sense what the Father's silence on the cross meant to Jesus and the abyss that was hidden in his

[75]

cry, 'My God, my God, why have you deserted me?' (Mt 27:46). Mary also knew what God's silence meant as she stood beneath the cross. No one more than Mary can understand the exclamation made by a Father of the Church while thinking about a time of ferocious persecution of the Church, under the emperor Julian, when churches were profaned and virgins raped: 'How hard it was that day, to endure your silence, O God!'

On the cross Jesus experienced to the end the fundamental consequence of sin, which is the loss of God. He became godless, the atheist! The word 'atheist' can have either an active or a passive connotation. It can indicate one who *refuses* God but also one who *is refused by* God. It is, of course, in this second meaning that the word 'atheist' applies to Jesus on the cross. His atheism was certainly not one of guilt, but one of pain. It expiated all the wilful atheism present in the world and in each of us in the form of resistance to God, egoism and indifference. Clearly, the Father was never closer to the Son than in that moment of his supreme obedience but, as man, for a moment, Jesus no longer felt the Father close, he 'felt' abandoned.

* * *

All this was necessary 'to destroy this sinful body' (Rm 6:6) and so that, in exchange for the curse, 'through faith we might receive the promised Spirit' (Ga 3:14). The Fathers applied to Christ on the cross the figure of the bitter waters of Marah which became sweet when Moses threw the tree into it (Ex 15:23 ff). On the cross Jesus swallowed all the bitter waters of sin, transforming them into the sweet waters of the Holy Spirit. He transformed the immense 'no' of men to God into an even more immense 'yes', *amen*. That is why 'it is 'through him' that we answer Amen to the praise of God' (2 Co 1:20).

'The mystery of our religion is very deep indeed' (1 Tm 3:16). It consists in the fact that even in such an extreme situation, Jesus kept his trust in God and his loving submission to the Father. His filial cry, 'Abba, Father!' never ceased and he died crying with a loud voice, 'Father, into your hands I commit my spirit' (Lk 23:46).

In fulfilling this mystery of our religion, Mary, the mother of Jesus, was close to him and we now lovingly turn our thoughts to her. A document of Vatican II says, 'She suffered grievously with her only-begotten Son. She united herself with a maternal heart to his sacrifice, and lovingly consented to the immolation of this Victim which she herself had brought forth.' For this reason she is 'a mother to us in the order of grace' (*Lumen Gentium* 58, 61).

* * *

In the New Testament, the kerygma of the passion is always made up of two elements: of a *fact* he 'suffered' and 'died', and of the *reason* for this fact, 'for us', 'for our sins' (Rm 4:25; 1 Co 15:3). Christ's passion is inevitably unrelated to us until we enter into it through the narrow door of this 'for us', because only he who acknowledges that Christ's passion is his work, really understands Christ's passion.

Therefore, my personal sin was also present on Gethsemane, weighing on the heart of Jesus; on the cross my egoism and my abuse of freedom kept him nailed. If Christ died 'for my sins', then – simply by making the phrase active – I killed Jesus of Nazareth! The three thousand whom Peter addressed at Pentecost had not all been present in Pilate's praetorium or on Calvary hammering in the nails, yet he lifted his voice and said to them, 'You crucified Jesus of Nazareth!' And by the work of the Holy

[77]

Spirit, they acknowledged it was true because it is written, 'they were cut to the heart and said to Peter and the apostles, "What must we do, brothers?" (Ac 2:23, 37).

'Were you there, were you there, when they crucified my Lord?', goes a Negro spiritual full of faith. And it goes on, 'Sometimes it makes me tremble, tremble, tremble'. Every time I hear it, I am compelled to think: 'Alas, yes, I was also there, I was also there, when they crucified my Lord!'

It is necessary that every man experience an earthquake once in his lifetime, and that he experience in his heart something similar to what happened in nature at the moment of Christ's death when the temple curtain was torn in two from top to bottom, the rocks split and the tombs were opened. It is necessary that a holy fear of God shatter, once and for all, our hearts which are so self-confident in spite of everything. Peter the apostle experienced something of this kind and he was able to cry out those tremendous words to the multitude because he had first cried them to himself and, when Jesus looked at him, he had 'wept bitterly' (Lk 22:61).

In the reading of the passion we have just heard these words from John's gospel, 'They will look on the one whom they have pierced' (Jn 19:37). May this prophecy be realised in us too; let us look on him whom we have pierced and mourn for him as one mourns for an only child (Zc 12:10). If the world is not converted by listening to us preachers of the Gospel, let it be converted by seeing us weep and mourn!

* * *

It is time that each one 'be baptised in his death', that something of the old man fall from us and remain buried for ever in the passion of Christ. Scripture says that the

time that is past should suffice for giving way to passions
(1 P 4:3). Let the time that is past suffice for justifying
ourselves and accusing others. Let there be an end of
pointless controversy between us Christians. Christ died
'to gather together in unity the scattered children of God'
(Jn 11:52), and should we continue to be divided and
dispersed for things of secondary importance? How can
we go on wasting ourselves on trivial differences of
opinion in front of a God who died for love of us and a
world, of which a great part still ignores him? *Cessent jurgia
maligna cessent lites,* 'Let all the sad disputes cease, let the
quarrelling cease and may Christ our God be among us',
an ancient Gregorian hymn says. A lot of the evil and
unhappiness afflicting families, communities, society and
the Church is caused by individual judgements and accusation of others, instead of first of all judging and accusing
oneself and one's sin; each one of us wants to change the
others, and only very few indeed seriously think about
changing themselves. For if we decided to put this revolu-
tion into practice in ourselves, the world would be a better
place this very night and there would be peace in our
hearts. If it were then necessary to defend truth and justice, we should be able to do it better and with greater
freedom and charity.

* * *

Only when we have been through this new sort of baptism
in Christ's death will the cross completely change aspect
for us and, instead of accusing us and being a cause of fear
and sadness, it will become a source of joy and confidence. There is no condemnation for those who are in
Christ Jesus (Rm 8:1). Condemnation has run its course
and benevolence and forgiveness have taken its place.
Instead, the cross becomes our boast and our glory, 'The

only thing I can boast about is the cross of our Lord Jesus Christ' (Ga 6:14). Here, 'boast' indicates joyful confidence together with profound gratitude to which man is raised in faith. This is the sentiment pervading this service and which inspires this hymn of passion time, *O crux ave, spes unica*, 'Hail O cross, one only hope'.

Yet how can we boast and glory in a suffering we have not experienced but which, on the contrary, we have caused? The reason is that now Christ's passion has become 'ours', our greatest treasure, the rock of our salvation. If before 'for us' signified 'for our sins', now that we have acknowledged and confessed our sin and have repented, it signifies 'for our sake'. 'For our sake God made the sinless one into sin, so that in him we might become the goodness of God' (2 Co 5:21).

10

Near the cross of Jesus was Mary his mother

'NEAR THE CROSS of Jesus stood his mother and his mother's sister, Mary the wife of Clopas, and Mary of Magdala. Seeing his mother and the disciple he loved standing near her, Jesus said to his mother, "Woman, this is your son!" Then to the disciple he said, "This is your mother!" And from that moment the disciple made a place for her in his home' (Jn 19:25–27). These are the words we have just heard during the reading of the passion. And the account of what happened comes to us from John, who was there beneath the cross with Mary. Not much information comes to us from such a direct and sure source as this. And on this Holy Friday, we want to pause and reflect on these words.

If Mary were 'near the cross of Jesus' on Calvary, it means she was in Jerusalem during those days and, if she was in Jerusalem, it means that she saw all that happened. She was present at the whole of her Son's passion; at the shouting of 'Barabbas, Barabbas!', at the *Ecce homo*! She saw her Son come out scourged and crowned with thorns, covered with spittle; she saw his naked body tremble in the death agony. She saw the soldiers divide his garments and cast lots for his tunic which she had lovingly woven. She also drank the bitter chalice to the end. The words of desolation of the ancient daughter of Zion are fitting for her, 'All you who pass this way, look and see: is any sorrow like the sorrow that afflicts me?' (Lm 1:12).

Mary was not alone by the cross; besides John, there were three other women with her: her sister and Mary the wife of Clopas and Mary of Magdala. It might seem that Mary was just one of the many women present. But she was there as 'his mother' and that was the difference, as it places her in a unique position compared with all the others. I have sometimes attended a young person's funeral and I am now thinking particularly of a young boy's funeral. Several women, all dressed in black and weeping, followed the hearse. They all seemed to be suffering in the same way. But there was one among them who was different. All the others were thinking of her, weeping for her and looking sideways at her. She was the young boy's mother. She stared fixedly at the coffin as if she were turned to stone and you could see her lips repeating her son's name over and over again. When, at the *Sanctus*, everyone started to repeat with the priest, 'Holy, Holy, Holy is the Lord God of the Universe . . .', she too started to murmur mechanically, 'Holy, Holy, Holy . . .'. At that moment I thought of Mary at the foot of the cross.

But Mary was asked for something much more difficult. She was asked to forgive those who had killed her Son. When she heard her Son saying, 'Father, forgive them; they do not know what they are doing' (Lk 23:34), Mary immediately realised what the heavenly Father wanted from her too, that she should repeat the same words in her heart, 'Father, forgive them . . .'. And she repeated them. She forgave.

* * *

Vatican Council II says of Mary at the foot of the cross, 'The Blessed Virgin advanced in her pilgrimage of faith, and loyally persevered in her union with her Son unto the cross. There she stood, in keeping with the divine plan, suffering grievously with her only-begotten Son. There she united herself with a maternal heart to his sacrifice, and lovingly consented to the immolation of this Victim which she herself had brought forth' (*Lumen Gentium* 58). To consent to the immolation of the Victim she herself had brought forth was to immolate herself.

Standing 'upright' by the cross, Mary's head was close to her Son's bowed head. Their eyes met. When he said, 'Woman, this is your son', Jesus was looking at her and therefore did not need to call her by name to distinguish her from the other women. Who could penetrate the mystery of that look between mother and Son at such a time? A tremendous painful joy passed between them and their joy sprung from the fact that they were no longer resisting pain, they no longer had any defences against suffering, they let themselves freely be immersed in it. Peace had taken the place of struggle. They had become one with the suffering and the sin of the whole world – Jesus directly as 'the sacrifice that takes our sins away, and not only ours, but the whole world's' (1 Jn 2:2), and Mary indirectly, through her spiritual and bodily union with her Son.

The last thing Jesus did on the cross before entering the dark moment of his agony and death was to adore the Father's will. Mary was with him in this too. She too adored the Father's will, before a dreadful solitude and darkness came over her heart just as there was darkness outside over all the land (Mt 27:45).

And that solitude and adoration remained fixed there,

[83]

at the centre of her life, until her death when the hour of resurrection came for her too.

A psalm that the liturgy applies to Mary says, ' "Here so and so was born" men say. But all call Zion "Mother", since all were born in her' (Ps 87:4). It is true: we were all born there; it will be said also of Mary, the new daughter of Zion, this one and that one were born in her. In the eternal records it is registered of you and me, of everyone, even those who do not yet know it: 'Here so and so was born'.

But were we not born through the living and abiding word of God (1 P 1:23)? Are we not 'born of God' (Jn 1:13), born of water and the Spirit (Jn 3:5)? This is all true, but it does not exclude the fact that, in a different way, we are also born of Mary's faith and suffering. If Paul, who was a servant of Christ, could say to his followers, 'It was I who begot you in Christ Jesus by preaching the Good News' (1 Co 4:15), how much more can Mary, who was his mother, say it? Who, more than her, can claim the apostle's words, 'My children! I must go through the pain of giving birth to you all over again' (Ga 4:19). She is in labour 'again' with us, at this moment, because she already once gave us life in the incarnation when she gave the world the 'living and abiding word of God' who is Christ, in whom we are born anew.

* * *

A comparison with Abraham can make the significance of Mary's presence by the cross clearer. It was the angel Gabriel himself at the annunciation who suggested this comparison when he spoke to Mary the same words that were said to Abraham, 'Nothing is impossible to God' (Gn 18:14; Lk 1:37). But it emerges especially from the facts. God promised Abraham that he would have a son even if he was too advanced in years and his wife was barren. And Abraham believed. God announced to Mary that she would bear a son even if she was a virgin. And Mary believed. But then God appeared again to ask Abraham to sacrifice the son he had given him and of whom he had said: 'Through Isaac you will have descendants.' And Abraham again obeyed. God appeared a second time in Mary's life too, asking her to consent, or rather, to assist the immolation of her Son of whom it had been said that he would reign for ever and would be great. And Mary obeyed. Abraham climbed Mount Moriah with Isaac and Mary followed Jesus up Mount Calvary. But much more was asked of Mary than of Abraham. God stopped Abraham at the last minute and restored his son to him, but not with Mary. She had to cross the final threshold of no return, the threshold of death. Her Son was restored to her, but only when he had been taken down from the cross.

As Mary's path was one of faith and not of vision, she hoped that the course of events would change from one minute to the next, that her Son's innocence would be recognised. In vain did she hope in front of Pilate. In vain did she hope along the way to Calvary. Abraham went ahead. She hoped right up to the cross, before the first nail was hammered in, but it was not to be. Had she not been promised that her Son would sit on the throne of David and would reign over the house of Jacob for ever? Was this cross therefore the throne of David? Mary indeed hoped and believed against hope (Rm 4:18); she hoped in God even when she saw the last human reason for hope disappear.

Let us now draw the due consequences from this comparison. If for what he did Abraham deserved to be called 'the father of all of us' (Rm 4:16), and 'our father in faith'

[85]

(Roman Canon), could we hesitate to call Mary 'mother of us all' and 'our mother in faith', or 'mother of the Church'? God said to Abraham, 'Because you have done this, because you have not refused me your son, your only son, I will shower blessings on you, I will make your descendants as many as the stars of heaven and the grains of sand on the seashore. . . . You shall become the father of a multitude of nations' (Gn 22:16–17; 17:5). And now, more strongly, he says the same thing to Mary, 'Because you have done this, and have not refused me your Son, your only Son, I will shower blessings on you. You shall become the mother of a multitude of nations!'

Believers of different Christian denominations hold the common conviction that Abraham was not just made 'an example and patron but also a cause of blessings' (as Calvin says in a commentary on Gn 12:3) and that 'in God's plan of salvation Abraham was given the role of mediator of blessings for all generations' (G. von Rad). Why, then, should all Christians not joyfully accept and share the conviction that God with even greater reason made Mary 'cause' and 'mediatrix' of blessings for all generations? Not only, I repeat, an example, but also a 'source of salvation', as St Irenaeus calls her (*Against Heresies* III, 22, 4)? Why shouldn't the conviction be shared that the words of Jesus as he was dying, 'Son, this is your mother' were addressed not only to John but to all the disciples? The council says that beneath the cross Mary has become 'a mother to us in the order of grace' (*Lumen Gentium*, 61).

So, like the Israelites, who in times of trial turned to God saying, 'Remember Abraham, our father!' we can now turn to him and say, 'Remember Mary, our mother!' and as they said to God, 'Do not withdraw your favour from us, for the sake of Abraham, your friend' (Dn 3:35), we can say, 'Do not withdraw your favour from us, for the sake of Mary, your friend!'

* * *

There comes a time in life when we need faith and hope like Mary's. It is when God no longer seems to hear us, when he seems to deny himself and his promises, when he makes us face one defeat after another and the powers of darkness seem to triumph on all sides; when, as the psalm says, it seems that 'his anger overcomes his tenderness' (Ps 77:9). When this hour arrives, remember Mary's faith and pray, 'Father, I no longer understand you, but I trust you!'

Perhaps God is asking someone to sacrifice, like Abraham, his 'Isaac' to him right now – in other words, the person or object, the plan, the foundation or office he holds dear, which God himself entrusted to him one day and to which he has, maybe, dedicated his life's work. This is the chance God is offering you to show him that he is dearer to you than anything else, dearer than his own gifts or even than the work you do for him. God tried Mary on Calvary 'to see what was in her heart' and in her heart he found the 'yes' and the 'Here I am' she uttered on the day of the annunciation intact and reinforced. May he now find our hearts ready to say 'yes' and 'Here I am'.

Mary, as I have said, joined her Son on Calvary in adoring the Father's will. Thus she realised to perfection her calling within the Church. She is now awaiting us there. It has been said that 'Christ is in agony to the end of the world and we must not abandon him in this time' (Blaise Pascal). And if Christ is on the cross in agony to the end of time, in a way that is incomprehensible for us, but true, where else could Mary be if not close to him 'near the cross'? It is there that she invites and welcomes generous souls so that they can join her in adoring the holy will of the Father. To adore it even without understanding it. We must not abandon her in this time. Mary knows that this is the greatest, most wonderful and most worthy thing we can do in life, at least once before our death.

It is written that when Judith went back to her people after putting her life at risk for them, the men of the city hurried to meet her and the High Priest blessed her saying, 'May you be blessed, my daughter, by God Most High, beyond all women on earth; ... The trust you have shown shall not pass from the memories of men' (Jdt 13:18 ff). Today we address the same words to Mary: Blessed are you above all women! Your trust and courage will never pass from the heart and memory of the Church!

11

He humbled himself

IN THE YEAR AD 630 Heraclius, emperor of Byzantium, having defeated the Persian King Chosroes, recovered the relics of the Holy Cross which Chosroes had taken away from Jerusalem fourteen years before. When he tried to replace the precious relic in the basilica that Constantine had erected on Calvary, a very strange thing happened which the liturgy commemorates on 14 September, the feast of the Exaltation of the Holy Cross. The Office of that feast-day used to tell us that 'Heraclius, completely covered in gold and precious stones, tried to go through the gate that led to Calvary but he could not move. The more he tried to move ahead, the more he felt nailed to the spot. There was general amazement. Then Zacharias, the bishop, mentioned to the emperor that perhaps his ornamental dress did not suit the humility with which Jesus Christ had crossed the same threshold carrying his cross. The emperor immediately took off his grand clothes and barefoot, in everyday clothes, he moved without difficulty to the spot where the cross was to be replaced.'

The rite which the pope performs when, without liturgical vestments and barefoot, he approaches the cross to kiss it, derives, in a remote way, from this episode. But there is also a spiritual and symbolic significance which concerns all of us here present, even those who do not approach the cross barefoot to kiss it. It signifies that we cannot possibly draw near to the cross unless we first get rid of our pretensions to greatness, to our rights; in other words to our pride and vanity. It is simply not possible; we would be invisibly rejected.

In this celebration we want to do just two simple things: first, to throw our personal load of pride and that of the world at the foot of the cross, and second, to put on the humility of Christ and with it return home 'justified', that is, forgiven, renewed.

* * *

In the book of Isaiah we can read:

> Human pride will be humbled,
> the arrogance of men will be brought low,
> God alone will be exalted,
> on that day. (Is 2:17)

'That day' is the day of Messianic fulfilment, the day Christ proclaimed from the cross: 'It is finished!' In short, that day is today! And how did God humble man's pride? By frightening him? By showing him his tremendous might and power? No, he humbled it by humbling himself.

> His state was divine,
> yet he did not cling
> to his equality with God
> but emptied himself,
> to assume the condition of a slave,

and became as men are:
and being as all men are,
he humbled himself (Ph 2:6–8).

He humbled himself, not mankind! He humbled the pride and haughtiness of men from within and not from outside. And how he humbled himself! Let us not be deceived by the splendour of this St Peter's Basilica, by the service, the singing, by all the honour surrounding the cross today. There was a time when the cross had nothing to do with all of this, but only with infamy. Something that, according to Cicero, Roman citizens had not only to be prevented from seeing but even from hearing about. He died as had been foretold, 'Without beauty, without majesty . . . despised and rejected by men, . . . a man to make people screen their faces; . . . we thought of him as someone punished, struck by God, and brought low' (Is 53:2–4). Apart from Jesus, only Mary, his mother, knows what the cross is really like. She bore with him the 'degradation' of the cross (Heb 13:13). Others, including St Paul, knew the power of the cross (1 Co 1:18), but she knew also its weakness; others have known the *theology* of the cross, Mary the *reality* of the cross.

The cross is the tomb which absorbs all human pride: 'Come thus far, I said, and no farther: here your proud waves shall break' (Jb 38:11). The waves of human pride break against the rock of Calvary and they can go no further. The wall God erected against them is too high and the abyss he dug before them too deep. 'We must realise that our former selves have been crucified with him to destroy this sinful body' (Rm 6:6). The body of pride – for this is the sin *par excellence*, the sin that gives rise to all other sins. 'He was bearing our faults in his own body on the cross' (1 P 2:24). He bore our pride in his body.

But what concerns us in all this? Where is the 'gospel', the good and joyful news? It is that Jesus humbled himself also for me, in my place. 'If one man has died for all, then all have died' (2 Co 5:14); one has humbled himself for all, therefore all have humbled themselves. Jesus on the cross is the new Adam obeying for all. He is the head, the beginning of a new mankind. He acts in the name of all and for the benefit of all. As 'by one man's obedience many will be made righteous' (Rm 5:19), so by one man's humility, many will be made humble.

Pride, like disobedience, is no longer part of us. It is part of the Old Adam. It has become old-fashioned. The new thing now is humility, which is full of hope because it opens up a new existence based on giving, love and solidarity and no longer on competitiveness, social climbing and taking advantage of one another. 'The old creation has gone, and now the new one is here' (2 Co 5:17). Humility is one of these marvellous new things.

What, therefore, does it mean to celebrate the mystery of the cross 'in spirit and in truth'? When applied to what we are celebrating, what is the significance of the ancient maxim: 'Acknowledge what you are doing, imitate what you are celebrating'? It signifies that you should implement within yourself what you represent externally; put into practice what you are commemorating in the liturgy.

This evening I must give Christ 'the sinful body of my pride', so that he can destroy it *de facto* just as he destroyed it by right once and for all on the cross. When I was a boy, the people of my region used to light a bonfire in the country at nightfall on the eve of certain feasts which could be seen over the hills. Each family would bring some wood and vine branches to keep the fire going while, around it, the rosary would be recited. Something

similar must take place here this evening in preparation
for the great feast of Easter. Each one of us should throw,
in spirit, his load of pride, vanity, self-sufficiency, presumption, haughtiness into the great furnace of Christ's passion. We must imitate the saints in heaven as they adore
the Lamb, for this is the model for our adoration here on
earth. Revelation tells us the saints approach the throne in
procession and fall down before him who is seated and
they 'threw down their crowns in front of the throne' (Rv
4:10). They cast the real crowns of their martyrdom, and
we cast the false crown with which we have crowned ourselves. We must 'nail all feelings of pride to the cross' (St
Augustine, *On Christian Doctrine* 2,7,9).

* * *

We should not be afraid of becoming dispirited, of relin-
quishing our dignity as human beings and thus fall into a
morbid state of mind. At the beginning of this century,
Nietzsche accused Christianity of having introduced the
'disease' of humility into the world. Now, philosophy itself
informs us that a 'genuine' human existence is based on
the awareness of our fundamental 'nothingness' (Martin
Heidegger, *Time and Being*, 58). Pride leads to desperation
because it means we do not accept ourselves as we are but
desperately want to be what we can never be, no matter
how much we try, that is, independent, self-sufficient, with
no one above us to have to thank for what we are
(Kierkegaard, *Sickness unto Death*).

Modern depth psychology reached the same conclusion
in another way. Jung made the amazing discovery that all
his patients of a certain age suffered from what could be
called a lack of humility, and there was no improvement
until they had acquired an attitude of respect and

humility towards a reality that was greater than themselves, in other words, a religious attitude.

Pride is a mask that prevents us from being truly human, even before being believers. It is human to be humble! The words *homo* and *humilitas* are both derived from *humus*, which means earth, soil. All that is not humility in man is part of the lie. 'Someone who thinks himself important when he is not, only deceives himself' (Ga 6:3).

* * *

As soon as we decide to cast off our pride we are shocked by the realisation of what a mixture of pride we are both inside and out. They say that over 70 per cent of the human body is made up of water, but perhaps even more than 70 per cent of man's spirit is made up of pride. The very air we breathe carries words and messages on all frequencies that are loaded with pride. There are even those who believe they can go 'beyond' Jesus Christ and openly declare a 'New Age', founded not on the incarnation but on the constellation Aquarius, not on the conjunction of divinity with humanity but on the conjunction of the planets. Every year new religions and new sects are founded and new ways of salvation are announced, as if the way revealed by God and founded on Christ was no longer sufficient for modern man, as if it were too humble for him. And what is this if not pride and presumption? St Paul said 'Are you people in Galatia mad? Has someone put a spell on you, in spite of the plain explanation you have had of the crucifixion of Jesus Christ' (Ga 3:1). O mad Christians! Who has put a spell on you, to make you pass so quickly to another gospel?

We all long to be noticed. If we could visualise the whole of humankind as it appears in the eyes of God, we would see the spectacle of an immense crowd of people all standing on tiptoe, all pushing one another in the attempt to make themselves seen and all shouting, 'I'm here too, I'm here in the world too!'

All this pride is, of course, just smoke that death dissipates day by day. 'Vanity of vanities', Scripture calls it. Not a gram of it will cross the threshold of eternity with us, and if it were to, it would soon condemn us. But its consequences are equally dreadful. It is like an atomic mushroom-cloud that rises threateningly into the sky like a closed fist and then falls back upon the earth causing destruction and death all around it.

What part did pride play in past and present wars, including that going on at this moment in the tormented former Yugoslavia? Does not the suffering of the poor depend in great part on the pride of certain heads of state who aim at more power and the security of their position and are therefore always in need of stronger armies and the most terrible arms? For this they are ready to invest the resources that should be used to improve the very often dreadful living conditions of their people. But also in daily living, in families and institutions, what awful suffering we cause one another through our pride and how many tears are shed because of it!

* * *

But we must not stop at this. It is not enough to denounce collective pride, which might simply be adding pride to pride. Our procession this evening must not be so much an exterior thing as interior. We must rend our hearts and not our garments (cf. Jl 2:13). It is in my heart that real pride is harboured, the only thing that I can destroy with my own will as it is the only thing my own will produces.

This is not an easy undertaking! The pearl diver of the

[95]

south seas who tries to go deep underwater experiences the tremendous resistance of the water which forcefully pushes him back up with a force that is equal and opposite to its volume. Without knowing it, he experiences Archimedes' principle. Whoever tries to dive below the calm water of his self-illusion, to humble himself and learn his true self, experiences the even stronger thrust of his own pride that tends to lift him above himself, so that he may emerge and remain on the surface. We too are looking for a precious pearl, the most precious in God's eyes. It is called a 'humble and contrite heart'.

How can we be contrite and humble of heart? Above all, let us seek the help of the Holy Spirit; let us lose the habit of defending ourselves and resisting. Let us look now, if we can, alone before God, into the mirror of our conscience. What pride, what vanity and self-complacency, what false humility and hypocrisy, in one circumstance or another, in one attitude or another. Maybe, alas, even now, at this very moment. How much 'I', 'I', 'I'. 'Blush, proud ashes, *erubesce superbe cinis*, God humbled himself and do you exalt yourself?' St Bernard used to say to himself (*Praise of the Virgin Mother*, 1, 8). St Augustine, before him, had said: 'Your Lord humble, and you proud? The head humble and the member proud?' (*Sermon* 354, 9, 9; PL 39, 1568).

Heaven and earth are filled with the glory of God; only man's heart is an exception, because it is filled with its own glory and not with God's. It is so taken with itself that it uses for its own glory even what was made for God. Even God himself! And yet, 'What do you have that was not given to you?' (1 Co 4:7).

To acquire a contrite and humble heart we need to be caught out once, like the woman in the gospel who was caught in the act of adultery, who stood there in silence with lowered eyes awaiting her sentence (Jn 8:3 ff). We are thieves caught in the act of stealing God's glory. If now, instead of fleeing elsewhere in thought or allowing ourselves to feel irritated, thinking, 'This is intolerable language. How could anyone accept it?' (Jn 6:60), we lower our eyes, strike our breasts and, like the tax collector, we say from the bottom of our hearts, 'God, be merciful to me, a sinner!' (Lk 18:13), then the miracle of a contrite and humble heart will begin to take place in us. And, like the woman, we shall experience the joy of forgiveness instead of condemnation. We shall have a new heart.

* * *

The multitudes who had assembled to see Christ's death 'went home beating their breasts' (Lk 23:48). How wonderful it would be to imitate them! How wonderful it would be if the scene of the three thousand were to repeat itself here. On the day of Pentecost they felt cut to the heart at the thought of having crucified Jesus of Nazareth and said to Peter and the apostles, 'What must we do, brothers?' (Ac 2:37). This would really be 'imitating what we celebrate'.

A contrite and humble heart is 'a proper sacrifice' to please God (Ps 51:19). Today, the Church does not celebrate the sacrifice of the Mass because today's sacrifice must be our contrite and humble hearts. God says, 'With heaven my throne and earth my footstool, what house could you build me, what place could you make for my rest? All of this was made by my hand and all of this is mine – it is the Lord who speaks. But my eyes are drawn to the man of humbled and contrite spirit!' (Is 66:1–2). A humble heart is God's paradise on earth, the house where he likes to rest and reveal his secrets.

All external events, however great, including those we have recently witnessed with the collapse of the communist regimes in Eastern Europe, are ambiguous, and no one can foresee whether one day we shall rejoice over them or be sorry. But this is not the case of a humble heart that converts to God. Nothing more important for God can take place on the face of the earth. It is something that is absolutely new and absolutely positive.

* * *

Now that we have at least mentally placed all our pride at the foot of the cross, we must quickly take the second step and put on Christ's humility. 'In your midst I will leave a humble and lowly people, and those who are left in Israel will seek refuge in the name of the Lord' (Zp 3:12–13). Christ on the cross was the beginning of this humble and poor people who trust in the Lord; now we must become virtually part of them in actual fact, just as with baptism we have become part by right.

Jesus tells us in the gospel, 'Learn from me, for I am gentle and humble in heart' (Mt 11:29). And what did Jesus ever do to call himself humble? Did he think lowly or talk lowly of himself? On the contrary, he proclaimed himself 'Master and Lord', one who is greater than Jonah, than Solomon, than Abraham, than everyone. What then did he do? He took 'the condition of a slave' (Ph 2:7). He did not *consider* himself small, nor did he *proclaim* himself small, but he *made* himself small to serve us. He made himself 'last of all and servant of all' (Mk 9:35). Christ was not afraid to compromise his divine dignity when he humbled himself to become a man like other men.

Christ's humility is made up of obedience as well as service, 'He humbled himself and became obedient to death' (Ph 2:8). Humility and obedience appear to be almost the same thing here. Jesus on the cross is humble because he offers no resistance to the Father's will. He 'gave God back his power'; he fulfilled the great 'mystery of piety'. Pride is broken by his submission and obedience to God and to the authority created by God. Has anyone here always and only argued with God as an equal? Has he ended up convinced that he can also play chess with God because he has always checkmated others? Has he ever really surrendered to God? He should do so before dying if he wishes to finally find peace of mind. He should remember what is written, 'It is a dreadful thing to fall into the hands of the living God!' (Heb 10:31). To fall, obviously, unrepented.

* * *

On the cross Jesus did not just reveal or practise humility; he created it too. True Christian humility consists in participating in Christ's inner state on the cross. St Paul says, 'In your minds you must be the same as Jesus Christ' (Ph 2:5); the same mind and not a similar one. Apart from this, many other things can be taken for humility which are really either natural inclination or timidity, or a liking for understatement, or simply common sense and intelligence, when they are not a refined form of pride.

Once we have put on Christ's humility, it will be easier, among other things, to work for Christian unity, for unity and peace naturally follow humility. This is also true in families. Marriage starts with an act of humility. A young man who falls in love and who on his knees, as was once the custom, asks a girl to marry him, makes the most radical act of humility in his life. He begs and it is as if he were saying, 'Give me yourself. Alone, I am not sufficient to myself, I need you!' We could say that God created humankind male and female to help them to be humble, not to be haughty and self-sufficient, and to discover the blessing of depending on someone who loves you. He inscribed humility in our very flesh. But, unfortunately, pride too often takes over again and the person we love has to pay for the initial need we had of him or her. Then a dreadful wall of pride rises between the two partners and their incommunicability extinguishes all joy. This evening, Christian spouses are also invited to place all resentment at the foot of the cross, to be reconciled to one another, embracing each other for the sake of Christ who, on this day on the cross, 'killed the hostility' (Ep 2:16).

The 'humble people' were represented at the cross by Mary, of whom Vatican Council II says, 'she stands out among the poor and the humble of the Lord who confidently await and receive salvation from him' (*Lumen Gentium*, 55). Let us therefore pray to her, 'O Mary, you are the first fruit of the humble people and of the remainder of Israel. You are the suffering Handmaid of the Lord beside the suffering Servant of the Lord, the new obedient Eve beside the new obedient Adam. Through your intercession, obtain for us from Jesus the grace to be humble. Teach us to "humble ourselves under God's mighty hand", as you humbled yourself. Amen!'

12

And Jesus cried with a loud voice and yielded up his spirit

THE EVANGELISTS MATTHEW and Mark describe the death of Christ like this, 'Jesus, again crying out in a loud voice, yielded up his spirit' (Mt 27:50; Mk 15:37): *kraxas phonè megale* in Greek, *clamans voce magna*, in Latin. This cry of Jesus as he died holds a great mystery which we cannot neglect. If it was uttered, it was meant to be heard; if it is written in the gospel, it is part of the gospel. All that had not been said or could not be said in words in the life of Jesus, is present in that loud cry. With it, Jesus emptied his heart of all that had filled it in life. It is a cry that pierces the centuries, louder than any human cry of war, of pain, of joy or of desperation.

It is not presumptuous to try to enter into the mystery of that cry. There is an objective, doctrinal reason for doing so, which is biblical inspiration. 'All Scripture is inspired by God' (2 Tm 3:16); 'When men spoke for God it was the Holy Spirit that moved them' (2 P 1:21).

Therefore someone, the Holy Spirit, who 'inspired' Scripture, knows the secret of that cry. He usually explains in one place what he has left unexplained in another; he explains in intelligible words what at other times he says with 'groans that cannot be put into words' (Rm 8:26). He is the single divine author behind the many human authors of the whole Bible.

St Paul says, 'The depths of a man can only be known by his own spirit, not by any other man, and in the same way the depths of God can only be known by the Spirit of God' (1 Co 2:11). Therefore, no one knows Christ's thoughts except the Spirit of Christ which was in him and who was his 'inseparable companion' in life (St Basil, *On the Holy Spirit*, 16). Jesus did everything 'in the Holy Spirit'. All his preaching was done 'in the Holy Spirit'. His loud cry on the cross was made 'in the Spirit'. It was not the simple cry of a dying man.

Now 'we have received the Spirit that comes from God to teach us to understand the gifts that he has given us' (1 Co 2:23), including what he bestowed on us with that loud cry.

* * *

In his Letter to the Romans St Paul writes, 'The love of God has been poured into our hearts by the Holy Spirit which has been given to us' (Rm 5:5). When St Paul wrote this, he was not referring to God's love in general, or in the abstract, but to an actual moment, to a precise historical event, which he immediately goes on to illustrate. 'We were still helpless when at his appointed moment Christ died for sinful men' (Rm 5:6).

Let us listen carefully to the whole message the Holy Spirit gives us through the apostle. I think that we are close to the abyss from which the dying Christ's loud cry came. 'We were still helpless when at his appointed moment Christ died for sinful men. It is not easy to die even for a good man – though of course for someone really worthy, a man might be prepared to die – but what proves that God loves us is that Christ died for us while we were still sinners. . . . When we were reconciled to God by the death of his Son, we were still enemies' (Rm 5:6–10).

The cry of Jesus on the cross was a birth cry. In that moment a new world was being born. The great dividing wall of sin was being demolished and reconciliation was taking place. It was therefore a cry of pain and love at the same time. 'He had always loved those who were his in the world, but now he showed how perfect his love was' (Jn 13:1). He loved them with his last breath! We get an idea of the divine power that charged this cry of Christ from what it immediately brought about in those actually listening to it. It is written that when the centurion who stood facing him saw how he had breathed his last, he said, 'In truth this man was a son of God!' (Mk 15:39). He believed.

All we have to do is hear that cry of love and let it move us deep down, let it change us. Otherwise Good Friday will pass in vain for us. As soon as Jesus had cried out, 'the veil of the Temple was torn in two from top to bottom; the earth quaked; the rocks were split; the tombs opened' (Mt 27:51). This was to indicate what should take place also in our hearts. God had nothing against the rocks. The 'rocks' that have to split are of a different kind; they are 'the hearts of stone' of those who have never been moved, or wept or even reflected.

Jesus well knew that there is only one key that opens closed hearts, and it is not reproach, or judgement, or threats, or fear or shame. None of these. It is only love. And this was the weapon he used with us. 'The love of Christ overwhelms us when we reflect that one man has died for all' (2 Co 5:14). The term St Paul uses for this, *synechei*, in a circular sense means, it controls us from all sides, it besieges us, it engulfs us; or in a more linear sense:

it chases us and gives us no respite, *urget nos,* as it used to be translated in Latin.

We must allow ourselves to be seized up into this embrace. 'Love is strong as death; . . . the flash of it is a flash of fire' (Sg 8:6). If only these flashes could touch us on this holy day, touch at least some of us and make us decide to finally surrender to God's love! When we are dealing with God it is more important to be seized than to seize. These things are revealed to children and kept hidden from the wise.

* * *

Let us therefore make time for the love of Christ to wrap itself round us and enter into us. Let us expose ourselves to this love as to the summer sun. What is the Redeemer's love like?

The first quality is that it is *love for enemies.* 'When we were reconciled, we were still enemies.' Jesus had said that 'A man can have no greater love than to lay down his life for his friends' (Jn 15:13). But we must pay attention to what the word 'friends' signifies here. John himself shows that there is a still greater love than this, greater than giving one's life for one's *friends;* it is to give it for one's *enemies.* So then, what does the term 'friends' mean here? Not those that love you but those that you love ('friends' has the passive sense of 'being loved', not the active sense of 'loving'). Jesus called Judas 'friend' (Mt 25:50) not because Judas loved him (he was going to betray him), but because he loved Judas. And what does the word 'enemy' signify? Not those you hate but those that hate you ('enemies', on the other hand, has the active sense of 'hating' and not the passive sense of 'being hated'). God hates no one. He does not consider anyone an enemy. Good and bad, we are all his children.

[104]

This is the highest peak, the Everest, of love. We cannot really picture a greater love than this. To die for the enemy, to love those who hate us and wish only to destroy us and are actually destroying us! 'Father forgive them. Father forgive them.' And we were the enemy; us sinners, us the ungodly; we who learned from Adam that dreadful 'self-love that, if necessary, drives us to be scornful of God' (St Augustine, *On the City of God* 14, 28). 'Ours were the sufferings he bore . . . and the Lord burdened him with the sins of all of us . . . he never opened his mouth' (Is 53:4,6,7).

O, our Redeemer, how you loved us, how you loved us! Do not permit us to return home for the umpteenth time without having grasped the mystery of this day. Touch our hearts and let us tell you with joy, 'You cried aloud to me, O God, and you broke my barrier of deafness, and now I thirst for you' (St Augustine, *Confessions* X, 27). May the cry of the dying Christ break the barriers of our deafness too. On a day like today, some centuries ago, a great mystic was intensely meditating on the passion when she heard within her these well-known words, 'My love for you was not a joke!' (Blessed Angela of Foligno).

* * *

The second quality is that it is *a real and lasting love*. The fire of this love has not burnt out, it is not something of the past, of two thousand years ago, of which only the memory lives on. It exists now, it is alive. If it were necessary, he would die again for us because the love for which he died continues unchanged. 'I am more a friend to you than such and such a one', Christ tells us, as once he told the great mathematician and theologian Blaise Pascal, 'I have done for you more than they; they would not have suffered what I have suffered from you, and they would

[105]

not have died for you as I have done in the time of your infidelities and cruelties, and as I am ready to do, and do, among my elect' (Pascal, *Pensées*, 553).

Jesus has run out of signs for his love. There is nothing more he can do to show his love, for there is no greater sign than to give one's life. But he has run out of signs only for his love, not of love itself. Now his love is entrusted to a special sign, a different one, a sign that is real, a person: the Holy Spirit. 'God's love – the love we now know – has been poured into our hearts through the Holy Spirit.' It is therefore a living and real love, just as the Holy Spirit is living and real.

Where the other evangelists say that Jesus 'uttered a loud cry and breathed his last', John says that Jesus 'bowed his head and gave up his spirit' (Jn 19:30). That is, he not only breathed his last but he gave the Spirit, the Holy Spirit, his Spirit. Now we know what was in the loud cry that Jesus gave us as he was dying. Its mystery has finally been revealed!

* * *

The third quality of the Redeemer's love is that it is *a personal love*. Christ died 'for us', St Paul told us. If we understand the 'for us' only in a collective sense we deprive it of some of its greatness. The numeric disproportion re-establishes a certain proportion of value. It is true that Jesus is innocent and we are guilty, that he is God and we are men; but, after all, he is just one and we are billions. It might seem more plausible that one should die to save the lives of billions. But this is not the case. He died 'for us' also means 'for each one of us'. It must be taken in a distributive sense as well as in a collective sense. As St Paul says, 'God loved me and sacrificed himself for *my* sake' (Ga 2:20).

Therefore, he did not love the masses but individuals, persons. He died also for me, and I must conclude that he would have died just the same even if I had been the only one on the face of the earth to save. This is a certainty of faith. Christ's love is infinite love because it is divine and not only human. (Christ is also God and we must never, even for an instant, forget this!) But the infinite cannot split into parts. It is all in all. Millions of particles are consecrated every day in churches. But each of these contains not only a particle of Christ's body but the whole Christ. It is the same with his love. There are billions of people and each one receives not only a particle of Christ's love but the fullness of his love, whole and entire. All of Christ's love is in me and also in my neighbour and this fact should make me respect him, and have regard and charity for him.

I too can say, 'He loved me and gave his life for me!' He knows his sheep by name and he calls them by name (Jn 10:3). No one is just a number for him. How new and true do God's words, through Isaiah the prophet, ring on the lips of Jesus on the cross, 'Do not be afraid, for I have redeemed you; I have called you by your name, you are mine. . . . Because you are precious in my eyes, because you are honoured and I love you' (Is 43:1,4). You are honoured because I love you: it is all expressed in the singular case here. How sweet these words would sound to those who feel miserable, worthless, abandoned by all, if only they were courageous enough to believe them!

'Nothing therefore can come between us and the love of Christ,' St Paul exclaims at this point, 'even if we are troubled or worried or being persecuted' (Rm 8:35–36). This discovery can change a man's life, the news that we must never tire of shouting out to people today. This is the only sure and steady fact in this world: that God loves us!

* * *

I have said that Christ's cry on the cross was a birth cry, but it was of a singular birth. Some time ago when I was abroad, I heard the sad news that a young wife who was expecting her first baby had a tumour. If she had undergone chemotherapy, the tumour would have been kept under control, but alas, she would almost certainly have lost her baby. A choice had to be made. Her family and public opinion wanted her to save her life, consoling her with the fact that she could have other children. But she was unshakable and refused to be cured. It became a national case and was covered in the press and on television, partly because the topic of abortion was being widely discussed in the country in question at that time. To avoid people's curiosity, the young woman left the town and went back to her parents' home. After a few days she gave birth to a lovely little girl and a week later she herself died.

I wonder what that child will feel when she grows up and hears this? Everything in life will seem like a trifle to her when compared to what her mother did. Sometimes we meet children whose mothers died giving birth to them. They seem different, as if they are protecting a mystery. They seem to know, or want to know, nothing about what happened, but, in fact, they listen very carefully to any memory or word spoken about their mother. They distinguish people by how they talk about their mother. Her death is inscribed in their hearts, for they were born out of it.

And so, we are that little girl; we are those children born of a death! 'Lord Jesus Christ,' the priest says before communion, 'Son of the living God, by the will of the Father and the work of the Holy Spirit, your death brought life to the world (*per mortem tuam mundum vivificasti*).' The cry of Jesus on the cross is the cry of one dying while giving life.

This 'maternal' view of the Redemption has the advantage of telling us something new that partly completes and corrects the 'juridical' view which is based on the idea of 'ransom'. In the case of a mother who dies in the act of giving birth, the link between her death and the life of her child is intrinsic, not external. It does not lie in someone else (in our case, the heavenly Father) who, taking that into account, gives life. In this case it really is true that life is born out of death: 'Your death brought life to the world.' But not even this explanation is enough by itself, without the other, more traditional, image of 'ransom'. In fact, a child before birth has done nothing against his mother, it is neither an 'enemy' nor 'ungodly', as we were before Christ gave us life.

*   *   *

What will our response to the revelation of Christ's love be? Let us not immediately rush into making proposals and trying to repay it. We would not be able to, and neither is it the most important thing to do today. There is something we must do first of all, the only way to show we have understood, and that is, to feel touched and moved by it. Let us not scorn deep feeling and emotion. When it genuinely comes from the heart, it is the most eloquent and worthy reaction we could possibly have when faced with great love or deep sorrow. A spirit of compassion is a sign that we no longer belong to ourselves. It is opening our intimate selves to another. That is why we are so discreet with it. But we have no right to hide our emotional involvement from the person causing it. It belongs to him, for he caused it and it is directed to him. Jesus did not hide from the widow of Naim or from the sisters of Lazarus the fact that he was deeply moved; in fact, 'he wept' (Jn 11:35). And are we ashamed to show him that we are deeply moved by his suffering?

Of what use is a spirit of compassion? It is precious because it is like a plough that breaks the hard crust of the soil so that the seed can sink deep into the earth. It is very often the beginning of a true conversion and a new life. Have we ever cried – or, at least, wished to cry – for Christ's passion? There are saints who wept their eyes out over this. 'I weep for the passion of my Lord,' St Francis of Assisi used to answer when he was asked the reason for so many tears. It is written, 'They will look on the one whom they have pierced; they will mourn for him as for an only son' (Zc 12:10; Jn 19:37). And this is not just a prophecy but a command, an order from God.

We have cried enough tears over ourselves, polluted tears, tears of self-pity. It is time to cry other tears. Tears of wonder, of joy, of gratitude. Tears of compassion even before tears of repentance. It is time to be 'born again through water and Spirit'. How often, when I hear the passion being commemorated or I am about to do so myself, Dante's well-known verse comes to my mind and I repeat it almost angrily to myself, 'What do you weep at, if you do not weep at this?' (*Inferno*, XXXIII, 42).

The liturgy of the Church gives us the example. At Easter it is full of feeling. 'Father, how wonderful your care for us! How boundless your merciful love! O happy fault which gave us so great a Redeemer!', exclaims the *Exultet*. Let us repeat it this evening now that we have commemorated the cry of Jesus as he died on the cross, 'O happy fault which gave us so great a Redeemer!'

13

God did not spare his own Son

GOD'S WORD HAS a gift to offer us this evening. So great is this gift that I am already saddened by the thought that I shall spoil it, and that I can really do nothing but spoil it. And so I want to give the gift, whole and entire, immediately to you. I want to pronounce his name and place it safely in your hearts before its fullness is dispersed in the effort to express it in words. The Father! The Father of our Lord Jesus Christ!

How I long to cry aloud this name purely and lovingly, from which 'every fatherhood, whether spiritual or natural, takes its name' (Ep 3:14). Only Jesus can talk of the Father. When Jesus spoke of the Father the disciples' eyes opened wide and they were filled with a longing, and Philip exclaimed, 'Lord, let us see the Father, and then we shall be satisfied!' (Jn 14:8).

Why are we talking of the Father today, the day of Christ's death? St Paul wrote, 'what proves that God loves us is that Christ died for us while we were still sinners' (Rm 5:8). And again, 'God did not spare his own Son, but gave him up to benefit us all' (Rm 8:32). This is a surprising statement. The fact that Jesus died on the cross is not, to the human mind, a sign of the Father's love, indeed it is a sign of his cruelty or at least of his rigid justice. And in fact, it is as if a knowledge of the Father, even for believers, is blocked by a host of human prejudices. Jesus would be right to repeat again today, 'Father, Righteous One, the world has not known you!' (Jn 17:25).

The difficulty of reconciling the heavenly Father's goodness with the death of Christ springs from a twofold series of facts. One series is theological and for this, I regret to say, we theologians and preachers are responsible. We have often in the past given a picture of the mystery of Redemption in these terms: by sinning, man was greatly in God's debt and God exacted payment. Christ, the Son of God, then appears on the scene and pays the great debt with his own blood. Then the Father, 'satisfied' (a dangerous word!) and 'appeased' (another dangerous word!), forgives. It is clear that with time such cold, juridical images could not but give rise to a feeling of secret repulsion towards the Father, who impassively waited in heaven for the price of the blood of his only Son to be shed.

The other series of difficulties are cultural, ones which are typically modern. Psychology has played its part in underlining the deviations associated with the father figure in human terms: masculinism, authoritarianism, paternalism . . . They say that every son has the secret desire to kill his own father. These ideas about human fathers were also transferred to the heavenly Father, with the consequence that a whole current of modern culture felt bound to side with Jesus against the Father, to the point where we reached the so-called 'theology of God's death'. It would seem that finally mankind realised its secret desire to kill the Father.

* * *

The principal cause of all this resentment is human suffering, the fact that man suffers and God does not. We are reminded of the proud statement of a pagan philosopher: 'God knows no suffering, man overcomes it!' (Seneca, *On Providence*). It is said that we cannot accept a God who permits the suffering of so many innocent children. And if we try to point out that Jesus suffered too, they reply, 'But that is the main point we are making! At least it is certain that he was innocent. Why did he have to suffer?' And so we reach the limit of aberration where we use Jesus as a sort of tool against the Father.

We must react to this, as any loving son would react whose father has been insulted. We must rediscover the true countenance of the Father, his silent and hidden countenance, and Good Friday is the most propitious occasion for doing so. St Paul therefore tells us, 'God did not spare his own Son but gave him up for us all.' There is a Sunday when the Church liturgy links this text with that of Genesis 22, and in all likelihood the apostle was doing the same. The text from Genesis talks of Abraham to whom God says, 'Because you have done this, because you have not refused me your son, your only son, I will shower blessings on you. . . . All the nations of the earth shall bless themselves by your descendants.'

Abraham, old as he was, walking in silence with his son towards Mount Moriah, was therefore the symbol of another father. He was the symbol of God the Father who accompanied Jesus on his journey to Calvary. When he was leaving the Upper Room, Jesus turned to his disciples and said, 'You will leave me alone. And yet I am not alone, because the Father is with me' (Jn 16:32).

Who could describe Abraham's feelings as he took his son up Mount Moriah to be sacrificed? Origen said that the most dangerous moment for Abraham was when, along the way, Isaac, in total ignorance of what was hap-

[113]

pening, turned to his father and said, 'Father, here are the
fire and the wood, but where is the lamb?' He had no idea
that he was to be the victim. The word 'father', says
Origen, was a real temptation for Abraham, and what violence he must have had to do to himself so as not to betray
himself and turn back! And when Jesus in Gethsemane
says, 'Father, everything is possible for you. Take this cup
away from me' (Mk 14:36), who can tell what effect these
words had on the Father's heart? Abraham would certainly have preferred a thousand times to die himself
instead of killing his son.

Therefore, the heavenly Father and his Son, Jesus, were
together in the passion and together on the cross. More
than to the wooden arms of the cross, Jesus was nailed to
his Father's arms, or, as it were, to his will. Just as, in
eternity, it is from the unutterable and joyful embrace
between the Father and the Son that the Holy Spirit pro-
ceeds, the gift of their mutual love, so now and for all
time, it is from that painful embrace of Father and Son on
the cross that the Holy Spirit flows, the gift of them both
for us. Jesus bowed his head and 'gave up his spirit' (Jn
19:30).

* * *

We might wonder if it is right to talk of God the Father
like this. Is is right to talk of God's suffering? Is God not
immutable, impassive, eternal? The early Christians used
to talk easily about God's 'passions' and suffering. They
used to say, 'If the Son suffered, the Father suffered too.
How could the Son have suffered without the Father suffering with him?' (Tertullian, *Against Praxean*, 29). To the
passion of the Son the compassion of the Father corre-
sponds. 'The Father himself, God of the universe, full of
forbearance, mercy and pity, surely suffers in some way?

Or, maybe, you ignore the fact that, when dealing with human affairs, he suffers a human passion? He suffers a passion of love.' These words were written by one of the Fathers of the Church who most jealously defended God's prerogatives and transcendence (Origen, *Homily on Ezekiel*, 6, 6).

Christ's passion is a historical revelation, a sort of epiphany of the mysterious passion of God's heart. The same passion that made him exclaim in the Old Testament the words that we shall soon hear in the *Improperia*, or *Reproaches:* 'My people, what have I done to you, how have I been a burden to you? Answer me' (Mi 6:3). God himself gives the answer to the question 'Why does God suffer?' in the opening words of the prophet Isaiah, 'I reared sons, I brought them up, but they have rebelled against me' (Is 1:2).

It is true that God's suffering differs from ours, because ours is always to some extent endured and forced on us, while God's is sovereignly free and does not compromise his incorruptibility and unchanging nature. It is 'the passion of the impassive,' as one of the Fathers defined it (St Gregory Thaumaturgus).

Biblical God is love, and 'without sorrow there is no living in love' (*Imitation of Christ*, III, 5).

Very soon, however, a new heresy arose which distorted the doctrine of God's compassion. It rejected any distinction in God between Father and Son; in other words, it rejected the Trinity. These heretics claimed that Father and Son were different names for the same person. Therefore, they were called Patripassians, or, those who attribute the passion to the father. This was a very different idea to the orthodox one which claimed that the Father, while remaining the Father, that is, a distinct person, participates in the Son's suffering who remains his Son. As a pretext for the error, God's suffering was no longer spoken of. This was also due to the fact that the new Greek culture in which the Church had to proclaim the Gospel did not comprehend an impassioned God involved in time and history.

For some time now things have been changing, perhaps because of the new and dreadful experiences man has had in the field of suffering. In line with the Bible and the most ancient of the Fathers, the most attentive theologians have started to concern themselves again with the question of God's suffering. 'The world must know that the revelation of a God who is love upsets all its ideas concerning the divinity' (H. de Lubac, *Histoire et esprit*, Paris 1950, ch. 5). In his encyclical *Dominum et Vivificantem*, Pope John Paul II says on this point that 'in the humanity of Jesus the Redeemer, the suffering of God is concretised' (No. 39).

* * *

Who is the ultimate cause of this suffering? Should we, like certain Greek philosophers, think that even above God himself there is a Necessity, a Fate, to which each and everyone submits? God forbid! God is God, and there exists nothing and no one above him. Where is the cause then? It is contained in these few words: God's love and man's freedom. Human parents who have suffered because of the corruption and ingratitude of their children (and there are many today) know what it means to be held in contempt by their own children. God had devised a wonderful plan of grace for man. But sin intervened; man broke with God, saying: *Non serviam*, 'I will not serve!' (Jr 2:20). They all abandoned the Father's house like so many prodigal sons. But the reality is even more wonderful than the parable. In fact, the eldest son in this case does not remain tranquil in his father's house. The only Son 'who was in the Father's heart' saw the Father's great desire to get back all his children who had gone astray and did not wait to be told to 'go and die for your brothers!' Instead, he himself said to the Father, 'You who wanted no sacrifice or oblation, prepared a body for me . . . Then I said, . . . "God, here I am! I am coming to obey your will so that everyone should be saved " ' (Heb 10:5–7). 'He wants everyone to be saved' (1 Tm 2:4).

The most perfect obedience forestalls an order and obeys a simple desire. Christ's obedience was like this. St Thomas wrote that God gave his Son up to death 'in that, by infusing love in him, he inspired him with the will to suffer for us' (*Summa Theologica*, III, 47,3). And St Bernard said, 'God the Father did not ask for the blood of his Son, he accepted it as an offering' (*Non requisivit Pater sanguinem Filii, sed accepit oblatum*) (*Against the Errors of Abelard*, 8, 21).

The mystery we are celebrating this evening springs from there, from the very heart of the Trinity; it is born of the Father's love for us and the Son's love for the Father. On leaving the Upper Room, Jesus said, 'The world must be brought to know that I love the Father and that I am doing exactly what the Father told me' (Jn 14:31). We have, therefore, every reason to exclaim in the words of the *Exultet*: 'Father, how wonderful your care for us! How boundless your merciful love! To ransom a slave you gave away your Son!'

So now we know the meaning of the words, God 'did not spare' his only-begotten Son. They mean that he did not spare him for himself, he did not keep him for himself as a jealous treasure. The Father not only received his Son's sacrifice, but he also made the sacrifice of giving us his Son! 'How great was your love for us, good Father,

[117]

for you did not even spare your own Son, but gave him up to save us sinners! How great was your love for us!' (St Augustine, *Confessions*, X, 43). And we were ready to flee from your presence, believing you hated us!

* * *

A child who is certain of his father's love will grow up strong, secure, happy and free for life. God's word wants to do this for us, it wants to restore this security to us. Man's solitude in this world cannot be overcome except by faith in God the Father's love. A well-known philosopher wrote that 'God's paternal love is the only steadfast thing in life, the real point of Archimedes' (Kierkegaard, *Journals*, III A, 73).

Observe a child out walking with his father, holding his father's hand or being swung around by him, and you will have the best picture possible of a happy, free child, full of pride. I read somewhere that once an acrobat did a stunt on the top floor of a skyscraper; he leant out as far as he could possibly go, supporting himself on the bare tips of his toes and holding his small child in his arms. When they came down someone asked the child if he'd been afraid and the child, surprised at the question, answered, 'No, I wasn't, my father was holding me!'

God's word wants us to be like that child. And reminding us that God did not spare his own Son for us, St Paul cries out joyfully and victoriously, 'With God on our side who can be against us? . . . Could anyone accuse those that God has chosen? When God acquits could anyone condemn? . . . Nothing therefore can come between us and the love of Christ, even if we are troubled or worried, or being persecuted, or lacking food or clothes, or being threatened or even attacked. . . . These are the trials through which we triumph, by the power of him who

[118]

loved us' (Rm 8:31–37). And Jesus tells us therefore to free ourselves of fear, of all cowardice, of all discouragement. Your Father knows you and your Father loves you, Jesus says. You were not given the spirit of slaves, to fall back into fear, but the spirit of children to cry out: *Abba*, Father!

Before such an incomprehensible love it comes spontaneously to us to turn to Jesus and ask him: 'Jesus, you are our elder brother; tell us what we can do to be worthy of so much love and suffering on the Father's part?' And from the height of his cross, Jesus answers us not with words but with facts: 'There is', he says, 'something you can do, something I also did, for it pleases the Father: have confidence in him, trust him against everything, against everyone, against yourselves. When you are in darkness and distress, when difficulties threaten to suffocate you and you are on the point of giving up, pull yourselves together and cry aloud, "Father, I no longer understand you but I trust you!" And you will find peace again.'

* * *

Today, we see a particular type of suffering which these words about the Father might alleviate. When the angel described John the Baptist's mission to Zechariah, his father, he told him that he would 'turn the hearts of fathers towards their children and the hearts of the children towards their fathers' (Ml 3:24; cf. Lk 1:17). We are in need of this conversion again. He, whose name, *diabolos*, means the one who divides and separates, is no longer content to put a nation against another nation, one social class against another social class, one sex against the other: men against women and women against men. He wants to strike deeper and put fathers against

[119]

their children and the children against their mothers and fathers. How much suffering and what sadness there is in the world because of this, and how many misdeeds and crimes that leave us dumbfounded!

This evening, we are commemorating the divine love of a father for his son and of a son for his father. From this mystery may the grace of healing spring for the Church and for the world, a grace of healing that will convert anew the hearts of fathers to their children and those of children to their fathers; that will touch hardened hearts. 'I am writing to you, fathers,' St John the Evangelist wrote to the Christians of his time, 'who have come to know the one who has existed since the beginning; I have written to you, children, because you already know the Father' (1 Jn 2: 13). At this moment, I too am talking to you, fathers and children. We must begin from God again so as not to succumb to evil; to find again the joy of being a father, a mother, a son or a daughter; the joy of being alive, of existing.

It is written that on the sixth day of creation God saw everything that he had made and beheld 'it was very good' (Gn 1:31). On the sixth day of the new creation week, which is Good Friday, God again looks at his creation and sees that, thanks to the sacrifice of his Son, it is all 'very good' again. 'May God find joy in his creatures' (Ps 104:31).

And if this sick world of ours raises cries of rebellion, blasphemy and malediction to heaven, let us instead, on this most holy day of the year, cry out from the bottom of our hearts and in the name of all men, St Paul's words, 'Blessed be God the Father of our Lord Jesus Christ!' (Ep 1:3). Blessed by God the Father! Blessed, blessed!

14

And he will come again to judge both the living and the dead

'JESUS OF NAZARETH ... they killed him by hanging him on a tree, yet three days afterwards God raised him to life.... And he has ordered us to proclaim this to his people, and to tell them that God has appointed him to judge everyone, alive or dead' (Ac 10:39–42). The account of the passion presents us with a Jesus who was being judged. The trials against him were multiplying: Annas, Caiaphas, Pilate. And that was not enough. The Roman procurator has withdrawn, the multitude has dispersed, the court is deserted, but the trial continues relentlessly. Today, too, Jesus of Nazareth is under trial. Philosophers, historians, film producers and simple theology students all feel capable of judging him as a person, his teachings, his messianic claim, his Church.

But Peter's words which we have just heard and those Jesus himself said before the Sanhedrin suddenly rise like a curtain allowing us to glimpse a very different scene. 'From this time onward you will see the Son of Man seated at the right hand of the Power and coming on the clouds of heaven' (Mt 26:64). What a contrast! Now, everyone is seated and he is standing there in chains; then, everyone will be standing and he will be seated at the right hand of

God. Now it is man and history judging Christ, then it will be Christ judging man and history. Ever since the Messiah made salvation possible by immolating himself on the cross like a lamb, he has become the universal judge. He 'weighs' man and people. Before him it is decided who will stand and who will fall. There is no appeal. He is the High Court of Justice. This is the unchanging faith of the Church which constantly proclaims in the Creed, 'And he will come again to judge both the living and the dead. And his kingdom will have no end.'

* * *

In the millions of years of life on earth, man has become accustomed to everything; he has adapted himself to all kinds of climates and immunised himself against all kinds of sickness. But there is something he has never become accustomed to and that is injustice. He still cannot accept it. 'The thirst for justice and confession shakes the very bowels of the earth which erupts and trembles like those movements and jolts in nature that gave rise to mountain chains' (Paul Claudel). Just as we need mercy, we may need justice even more. It is not only God who wants it, but, paradoxically, man wants it too; even the ungodly want it. 'On the day of universal judgement, it is not only the judge who will descend from heaven, but the whole earth will hasten towards him' (Paul Claudel).

Good Friday is a suitable occasion to bring to mind again the truth about the last judgement, without which the whole world and all history would become incomprehensible. To someone visiting St Peter's Square for the first time, the Bernini colonnade appears somewhat confused. The four orders of columns that surround the square all appear asymmetric, almost like a forest of huge trees planted there haphazardly. But there is a certain point, marked by a circle on the ground, where we should stand and, seen from this point, the whole view changes completely. It all looks beautifully harmonious; the four orders of columns fall into line as if by magic, as if they were forming a single column. It is symbolic of what is taking place in the bigger square of the world where everything seems confused, absurd, the fruit more of a passing whim than of a divine providence.

The wise man of the Old Testament noted this also when he said, 'But I still observe that under the sun crime is where the law should be, the criminal where the good should be' (Qo 3:16). And, in fact, wickedness has always been seen to triumph and innocence to be humiliated. But as Bossuet pointed out, at times the opposite takes place which prevents us from thinking that there is something fixed and sure in this world, and then we witness innocence on the throne and wickedness on the scaffold. And the wise man of the Old Testament reached this conclusion, ' "God" I thought to myself "will judge both virtuous and criminal, because there is a time here for all that is purposed or done" ' (Qo 3:17). He too had discovered the right viewpoint: God's judgement.

* * *

'Men only die once, and after that comes judgement' (Heb 9:27). How human affairs change when seen from this angle, even those in progress today! Every day we hear or read of atrocities aimed at the weak and defenceless, which go unpunished. We witness Mafia people being accused of dreadful crimes defending themselves with a smile, able to fool the courts and judges and feel safe because proof of their crimes is not forthcoming. It is as if they had solved everything because they are able to get away with it before human judges. But, my poor brethren, you have not managed to get away with anything! The real judgement is still to come. Even if you should end your days in freedom, feared, honoured, even having a splendid religious funeral after you have bequeathed large sums of money for works of mercy, you have still not managed to get away with anything. The real Judge is still waiting for you on the other side of the threshold, and he cannot be fooled. God is incorruptible. It is a fearful thing to fall, in this state, 'into the hands of the living God' (Heb 10:31).

We know how judgement will take place. 'Next he will say to those on his left hand, "Go away from me, with your curse upon you, to the eternal fire prepared for the devil and his angels. For I was hungry and you never gave me food; I was thirsty and you never gave me anything to drink; I was a stranger and you never made me welcome, naked and you never clothed me, sick and in prison and you never visited me' (Mt 25:41–43). What will become then of those who not only did not give food to the hungry but even took it from them; of those who not only did not welcome the stranger but made him a stranger, an exile, a wanderer; of those who not only did not visit the prisoner, but who unjustly imprisoned him, kidnapped, tortured and killed him?

* * *

There are other things in our society which concern all of us. We have recently seen how it is possible for a general atmosphere of lawlessness to be established, in which it becomes a sort of competition to break the law, to corrupt and be corrupted, with the excuse that everyone does the same, that it is a routine procedure, the system. But meanwhile the law has never ceased to exist. And so, one day, someone begins to investigate and the result is a political cataclysm.

It is the topic of conversation on everybody's lips nowadays. But who stops to reflect that, in actual fact, this is the situation we are all living in, those investigating and those being investigated, before God's laws? We light-heartedly break God's commandments, one after the other, including that which says do not kill, with the pretext that everyone is doing it anyway, that society, progress, even civil law, allow it. But God never intended to abrogate either the commandments or the Gospel, and this general atmosphere of impunity is unreal and a dreadful illusion. What we are witnessing in the '*clean hands*' operation is a pallid picture of another much more dramatic enquiry pending on all of us. But who even thinks of this?

On a political level we react indignantly to the proposal of wiping the slate clean, and cancelling all penal responsibility. But on a spiritual level this is what we tacitly expect of God, that he will wipe out everything. A merciful God is not enough for us, we also want an unjust God who endorses injustice and sin. After all, we say, God is good and forgives everything. Otherwise, what kind of God would he be? And we do not reflect that if God were to come to terms with sin, the distinction between good and bad would collapse and with it the whole universe.

* * *

We must not let the words that past generations have handed down to us fall into oblivion: *Dies irae dies illa*, 'Day of wrath, that day. . . . There will be trembling and fear when the Judge appears to severely judge all.' *Liber scriptus proferetur*, 'The book will be opened in which is written what the world will be judged on.' Which book? First and foremost the 'written book', Scripture, God's word. 'The word itself that I have spoken will be his judge on the last day', Jesus said (Jn 12:48). And then, especially for those who have not known Christ, the book of one's own conscience. A book that, like a diary, will come out of the tomb with man. 'Every secret will be revealed, nothing will go unpunished', *nil inultum remanebit.* It will be the end of all human rebellion. 'Not a single stone here will be left on another' (Mt 24:2).

What has happened to the Christian people? There was a time when these words were listened to with holy fear. Now people go to the opera house, they listen to Verdi's or Mozart's *Requiem*, they love the notes of the *Dies irae*, they emerge, perhaps, humming or gesticulating to the music. But it never crosses their minds that those words concern them personally, that they are also talking about them.

Or people enter the Sistine Chapel here in the Vatican and sit and gaze breathless at Michelangelo's *Last Judgement*. But at the representation, not at the reality being represented! Adulterers, the ambitious, the ungodly, all sit there and exchange comments on the painting. But it does not enter their heads that one of those faces with their eyes full of terror has anything to say to them personally. Michelangelo himself was subjugated by the reality ('Come you blessed . . . Depart you wicked'), and we are content with his representation.

* * *

Much has been said of the restoration of Michelangelo's *Last Judgement*. But there is another last judgement that has to be restored as soon as possible, which is not painted on walls or bricks but in the hearts of Christians. That too, in fact, has faded and is falling to pieces. 'The hereafter (and the last judgement with it) has become a joke, an exigency so uncertain that not only does no one any longer respect it but no one even envisages it, so that people are actually amused at the thought that there used to be a time when this idea transformed everyone's existence' (Kierkegaard, *Concluding Postscript*, II, sect. 2, ch. 4). In some of the old basilicas the last judgement was depicted on the back walls opposite the altar, behind the congregation and not in front of it. This was so that the people could see it and remember as they emerged from the church into daily life. The idea of the judgement moulded their whole existence.

When I was a boy I saw a scene of a film that I have never forgotten. A railway bridge collapsed over a river in flood. On both sides sections of the track were hanging in the air. The guard of the nearest level crossing realised what had happened and raced towards the train that was approaching at full speed. It was getting dark, so he ran between the tracks waving a lantern and shouting frantically, 'Stop, stop; go back, go back!'

That train represents us vividly. It is the picture of a society going on carelessly to the rhythm of rock 'n' roll, intoxicated with its conquests and unheeding of what lies ahead. The Church must act as the guard did, as it were, and repeat the words Jesus spoke one day at the news that several people had lost their lives, 'Unless you repent you will all perish as they did' (Lk 13:5). Or the words the prophets spoke in their day, 'Repent, renounce all your sins, avoid all occasions of sin! . . . Why are you so anxious to die, House of Israel?' (Ezk 18:30–31). This could be one of the starting-points for a new evangelisation.

Someone might try to console himself with the thought that, after all, judgement day is still far off, perhaps millions of years away. Jesus again gives the answer in the Gospel, 'Fool! This very night the demand will be made for your soul' (Lk 12:20). Truly, 'the Judge is already to be seen waiting at the gates' (Jm 5:9). The last breath is hardly drawn before judgements takes place. A flash and the truth about everything is clear. Theology calls it the 'particular judgement', but it is none the less final. There can be no revision.

* * *

I must now clear up a possible misunderstanding. For whom does the bell toll? Who do these words on judgement summon? Are they for unbelievers only, for those outside? Certainly not! The Apostle Peter says, 'The time has come for the judgement to begin at the household of God; and if what we know now is only the beginning, what will it be when it comes down to those who refuse to behave God's Good News?' (1 P 4:17). Therefore, judgement begins with the Church, for of him who has been given more, more will be asked. Even in the Church there are those who do not serve God but who make use of him. Then, there will be no further distinctions, even between the teaching Church and the learning Church, between shepherds and the sheep. There will be room only for the distinction between the 'sheep' and the 'goats', that is, between the righteous and the wicked. The bell, or trumpet, of judgement sounds therefore for everyone. 'God has no favourites' (Rm 2:11). 'All the truth about us will be brought out in the law court of Christ' (2 Co 5:10).

In Matthew's gospel we read that when the chief priests had taken up the thirty pieces of silver that Judas had thrown down in the temple, they said, 'It is against the Law to put this into the treasury; it is blood-money' (Mt 27:6). I fear that in some places, we, the ministers of the Church, have not been sufficiently attentive and, unknowingly, money and offerings that were 'blood-money' have

[128]

sometimes ended up in the treasury of the temple. And therefore not only the last judgement but also the present one must begin with God's house!

* * *

Why should this severe reprimand be given during the Good Friday liturgy? Because the judgement has been anticipated by Christ's death. 'Now sentence is being passed on this world,' he said as his passion drew near (Jn 12:31). The last judgement will only be the revelation and application of this irrevocable judgement, of the absolute 'No!' pronounced by God to all the sin in the world. If we so wish, however, there is now a sure way of escaping a future judgement and assuring ourselves, in anticipation, of a favourable outcome, and that is by submitting ourselves to the judgement of the cross. The future Judge is now before us as Saviour and King. There is an essential difference between a king and a judge. A king has the *right* to spare someone if he so wishes; a judge has the *duty* to apply the law, even if he does not wish to.

Jesus 'has overridden the Law, and cancelled every record of the debt that we had to pay; he has done away with it by nailing it to the cross' (Col 2:14). Let us therefore place on the arms of the cross all the evil we have done, that 'written scroll' we carry within ourselves and which is ready to accuse us. Let no one return home with the will to go on sinning and with unrepentance in his heart. Let us judge ourselves so as not to be judged by God. He who accuses himself will be excused by God; and he who excuses himself will be accused by God. Let us leave here on Calvary all rebellion, every rancour, every impure habit, all avarice, all envy, every wish to do justice by ourselves. Let us forgive one another, for it is written that 'there will be judgement without mercy for those

[129]

who have not been merciful themselves' (Jm 2:13). Let us celebrate Easter by going through this new 'Red' sea of the blood of Christ.

The invitation is for everyone, even those outlawed as 'monsters' by society, though I do not know by what right. With Jesus, on Calvary, there were two thieves; one died blaspheming and the other died asking forgiveness. The memory of the first thief is still today a source of fear, while that of the second thief is a source of blessing and hope. To these people I say: Today, you have the chance of choosing which of the two you will represent tomorrow for your children, for society and for history. God is waiting for you to become a sign of the power of his grace. 'There is joy in heaven for one sinner who repents.' But this means true repentance for having offended God and injured society, and not only to obtain a reduction of punishment. Give this joy to God.

* * *

At a certain point the *Dies irae* changes tone; the trembling becomes a yearning prayer that might have been written for this day of the year. *Recordare, Jesu pie, quod sum causa tuae viae,* 'O good Jesus, remember, it was for me you came on earth. Do not condemn me on that day. You redeemed me on the cross; may so much sorrow not be in vain.' *Rex tremendae maiestatis, qui salvandos salvas gratis, salva me, fons pietatis,* 'O King of great majesty, who freely save those who are destined for salvation, save me, fount of mercy.' Save all of us, when you come again in glory to judge the living and the dead.

15

Christ loved the Church and gave himself up for her

'ONE OF THE soldiers pierced his side with a lance; and immediately there came out blood and water' (Jn 19:34). At one stage, when reflecting on these words, it was as if the ancient Church was dazzled by a revelation. St John Chrysostom exclaimed, 'My beloved, do not be hasty to pass over this mystery because I have a mystical interpretation to lay before you. The blood and water are symbols of baptism and the Eucharist from which the Church was generated. Therefore, the Church was formed from Christ's side just as Eve was formed from Adam's side. . . . And as he then took Eve from Adam's side while he slept, so now, after his death, he gave blood and water. Death is now what sleep was then. Can you see how Christ united the Spouse to himself?' (*Baptismal Catecheses*, 7:17–18).

In the West, St Augustine echoed these thoughts. 'The first woman was formed from man's side while he slept, and she was called life and mother of the living. Here, the new Adam bowed his head and slept on the cross, so that from the blood and water that flowed from his side, his Church would be formed' (*On the Gospel of John*, 120, 2).

All of this helps us to see the liturgy we are celebrating in a new light. At first sight we might think that the Good

Friday liturgy belongs to, or was inspired by, the *threnoi* ritual, that is, the lamentations that were said for a dead person; or to the *epinikion* genre with which a victory was celebrated. Both are true. We weep over a dead person and celebrate a victory because on the cross 'the Lion of the tribe of Judah . . . has triumphed' (*enikesen*) (Rv 5:5).

But the Good Friday liturgy is above all an *epithalamium*, a nuptial hymn. In the Bible there is a psalm known as a royal wedding song which was composed for the wedding of the son of a king and queen, and which tradition has applied to Christ and the Church. It begins with these words: 'My heart is stirred by a noble theme; I address my poem to the king.' To the bridegroom it is said, 'Of all men you are the most handsome', and to the bride, 'Forget your nation and your ancestral home, then the king will fall in love with your beauty' (Ps 45).

But there is also an *epithalamium* in the New Testament which was written precisely for this new wedding of Christ to his Church. It is the Letter to the Ephesians, and it tells us, 'Husbands should love their wives just as Christ loved the Church and sacrificed himself for her to make her holy. He made her clean by washing her in water with a form of words, so that when he took the Church to himself she would be glorious, with no speck or wrinkle or anything like that, but holy and faultless. . . . A man never hates his own body, but he feeds it and looks after it; and that is the way Christ treats the Church. . . . For this reason, a man must leave his father and mother and be joined to his wife, and the two will become one body. This mystery has many implications; but I am saying it applies to Christ and the Church' (Ep 25–32).

* * *

There is a significant progression in the idea of the

Church in the Letter to the Ephesians, a sort of effort to reach an ever deeper understanding of the mystery she presents. From the beginning she is presented in the image of a building, as 'the household of God', Christ Jesus himself being 'its main cornerstone' (Ep 2:20). The relation between Jesus and the Church is likened to that between the foundations of a house and the house itself. Further on the Church is presented as the 'body of Christ'. We read that God established that some should be apostles and some prophets, 'building up the body of Christ' (Ep 4:11–12). Here the relationship is likened to that between the head and the body. 'We shall grow in all ways into Christ, who is the head' (Ep 4:15).

But St Paul still seems unhappy with these images of a building and a body, and so he gives us another: the 'spouse'. When Adam saw Eve he exclaimed, 'This at last is bone from my bones and flesh from my flesh' (Gn 2:23). And that is what Christ now says of his Church.

Where is the difference? The building is not a partner, an interlocutor, with whom one can talk. Neither is it a person who stands before me with his freedom, whom I can love and be loved by. The spouse is all of this! Also the new Adam was looking for 'a help like to him' and he got it!

* * *

At his point I must make use of the words spoken by St John Chrysostom and say, 'Do not be hasty to pass over this mystery, because I have a mystical interpretation to lay before you.' St Paul's affirmation that 'Christ loved his Church' implies a question that echoes all round us. Christ loved his Church: what about you? Do you love the Church?

'A man never hates his own body', that is, his spouse,

and Christ does least of all. Then, my brother, why do you say, 'God yes, but the Church no'? Why do you so easily point an accusing finger at your mother, saying, 'The Church is wrong about this, the Church is wrong about that; the Church should say; the Church should do . . .'? Who are you to dare to point at the spouse I love? says the Lord. 'Where is your mother's writ of divorce by which I dismissed her?' God says through Isaiah the prophet (Is 50:1). I think these words are addressed to many Christians today, 'Where is it written that I have divorced your mother, the Church, that she is no longer my spouse?'

The Church is also 'the stone the builders rejected' (the builders of our modern secular society). She is 'the repudiated spouse', but repudiated by man and not by God. God is faithful. In some parts of the world there is a term, the 'unchurched', Christians without a Church, that describes this kind of believer. And they do not realise that in this way they not only deprive themselves of the Church, but also of Christ (unless ignorance or good faith excuses them). What Jesus said of every marriage is even more applicable to his marriage with the Church: 'What God has united, man must not divide' (Mt 19:6).

Whoever does not love the Church (at least when he has come to know her) does not love Christ. St Cyprian said that 'Whoever does not have the Church as mother cannot have God as Father' (*On the Unity of the Church*, 6). For the Church to be your mother does not just mean that you were once baptised into the Church; it also means to consider, respect and love her as a mother and show solidarity with her in good and bad.

If you look at the windows of an old cathedral from the street, you will only see pieces of dark glass held together by strips of black lead; but if you cross the threshold and view them from inside, against the light, you will see a breathtaking spectacle of colours and shapes. It is the same with the Church. Whoever sees it from the outside, with the eyes of the world, will see only its dark and miserable side. But from the inside, with the eyes of faith and a sense of belonging, you will see what St Paul saw, a wonderful building in which the whole structure is joined together, a spouse with no defects, a 'great mystery'!

* * *

Perhaps you are thinking, 'And what about all the incoherence in the Church? And the scandals, even those of certain popes?' This is because you are reasoning in a human way, as a person of the flesh, and you cannot accept that God manifests his power and love through weakness. As you have been unable to reach innocence, you exact it from the Church, whereas God decided to manifest his glory and omnipotence through the awful weaknesses and imperfections of men, including the 'men of the Church', and with these he formed his spouse, which is wonderful, simply because she exalts his mercy. The Son of God came into this world and, good carpenter that he became under Joseph's training, he gathered together the most rickety and knotty pieces of wood that he could find and he built a ship which is still afloat after two thousand years (Bruce Marshall).

The sins of the Church! Do you really think that Jesus does not know them better than you do? Did he not know for whom he was dying? And where were his apostles then? But he loved this real Church, not an imaginary and ideal one. He died 'to make it holy and pure' and not because it *was* holy and pure. Christ loves his Church 'in hope'; not only for what she 'is', but also for what she 'will become', the new Jerusalem 'as beautiful as a bride all dressed for her husband' (Rv 21:2).

Have we ever asked ourselves why this Church of ours is so miserable and slow? Father Primo Mazzolari, who was certainly not in the habit of flattering the institutional Church, wrote, 'Lord, I am your poor flesh; I'm as much a weight as any cross, as a shoulder that cannot take the weight. So as not to leave me on the ground, you take up my burden too and walk as best you can. And some of those you carry accuse you of not walking according to the rules and even accuse your Church of slowness, forgetting that, burdened as she is with human misery which she does not want to get rid of and cannot (they are her children!), carrying them is worth much more than actually arriving somewhere.' It is true that the Church moves slowly. She is slow in the process of evangelisation, in following the signs of the times, in the defence of the poor and in many other things. And this is because she is carrying all of us on her shoulders and we are still a dead weight of sin. Children criticise their mother for being full of wrinkles, not realising that they themselves are the cause of these wrinkles, as so often happens in the natural order. Christ loved the Church and gave himself for her so that she would be 'without fault', and the Church would be without fault if we were not there! The Church would have a fault less if I had committed one sin less. To a reformer who reproached him for remaining in the Catholic Church in spite of its 'corruption', Erasmus of Rotterdam answered: 'I bear with this Church in the hope that it will improve, just as it is obliged to bear with me in the hope that I will improve.'

* * *

We must ask God's forgiveness for the many thoughtless judgements and offences we have caused his spouse and, consequently, him too. Try telling a man in love that his spouse is ugly or that she is of 'loose morals' and you will see how offended and angry he becomes.

We must all adopt a new and more responsible way of talking about the Church. 'As I am one of them,' Saint-Exupéry wrote of his homeland, which was going through a dark period, 'I shall not repudiate them whatever they might do. I shall not preach against them in front of strangers. I shall defend them if it is possible to do so. If they shame me, I shall hide it in my heart and keep silent. Whatever I think of them, I shall never bear witness against them. A husband does not go from house to house informing his neighbours that his wife is a harlot; he would not save his honour like that. As his spouse belongs to his house, he cannot diminish her to make himself appear superior. Instead, when he goes back home, let him then give vent to his anger' (*Pilote de guerre,* 24).

There is the risk that someone might do exactly what Saint-Exupéry is condemning here. It would be the case of someone leaving the Church and then going from university to university, from newspaper to newspaper, from congress to congress, giving voice to his bitter accusations against the 'institutional' Church, as if this were a completely different thing to his ideal of the Church, thinking he can save his own honour by presenting the Church in a bad light. We know that the world thinks wonders of those who leave the Church. Speaking of those who abandon the Church for some heretical sect which immediately confers honour and rank on them, Tertullian said, 'How easy promotion is when you pass over to the enemy's side!' (*Against Heretics,* 41, 7). It is often the case that one hides one's total loss of faith behind a thick cloud of accusations against the Church.

Should everyone always keep silent then in the Church? No. Once you have 'returned home', once you have wept for the Church, once you have humbled yourself beneath her feet, God may command you, as he did with others in the past, to raise your voice against the 'scars of the Church'. But not before then, and not without this risky mission causing you some form of death.

The saints have applied to the Church what Job (in the Vulgate translation) said to God: 'Should he kill me, I will continue hoping in him' (Jb 13:15).

* * *

From all that we have contemplated on this Good Friday, we now raise a particular appeal for consecrated souls. They are 'wedded' to the cause of the Kingdom. Out of pure grace they felt the need of 'something majestic' to love, and they found it in Christ. That is why they are called to be a visible sign of the nuptial love between the Church and Christ.

There is a lot of talk today about a certain unease in the traditional religious life, of an identity crisis. The approaching Synod of Bishops will try to analyse this and reach conclusions, as the theme for the synod is 'Consecrated life and its mission in the Church and in the world'. I think there are many explanations for this unease, but the main one is that many of us have lost the enthusiasm of our love for Christ, who is the reason for our choice.

The Book of Revelation contains a letter for us religious. It was written to the Church in Ephesus and it says, 'I know all about you; how hard you work and how much you put up with. . . . Nevertheless, I have this complaint to make; you have less love now than you used to. Think where you were before you fell; repent' (Rv 2:2–5). We, too, are often left with the works, the toil and the patient endurance (all precious and not to be neglected), but perhaps the spirit, our nuptial love for Christ, has gradually weakened. Love needs prayer if it is to survive, just as the fire needs oxygen if it is to blaze. 'If anyone has ears to hear, let him listen to what the Spirit is saying to the churches' and, I would add, to religious communities today.

* * *

Finally, from what we have contemplated today, we also raise an appeal for Christian spouses. St Paul himself wrote: 'Wives should regard their husbands as they regard the Lord. . . . Husbands should love their wives just as Christ loved the Church' (Ep 5:22,25). (Today we would say that wives must also 'love' their husbands.) Women should not feel diminished if in the symbolism used they represent the Church, and men represent Jesus Christ. They should feel honoured by the fact that all mankind is represented here by a woman, by Eve who is the Church. In practical terms, men are not represented here by Christ, but by the Church; they are not the groom but the bride.

This is the international year of the family, and the Church makes every effort to defend its rights and promote its holiness. But the family will not be healthy if the relationship between a couple is unhealthy. This is the decisive factor. When the relationship between a couple breaks down, it is like when the rope of a party of mountaineers breaks and all those roped together are hurled into the abyss. The children are the first to experience this.

What can a Christian couple learn from the Christ—Church model? There is one particular thing they can learn. Two kinds of love exist in the world: a munificent love and a love made up of suffering. The first kind consists of making gifts and offerings to the beloved; the second of being able to suffer for, or because of, the beloved. With creation, God loved us with a munificent love, but on the cross he loved us also with a suffering love, which is infinitely more exacting.

So as not to think, however, that it is all and only suffering, let us not forget what Jesus once said. 'There is more happiness in giving than in receiving' (Ac 20:35). Joy in discovering a whole new plane of love, to love as God loves, to know a love that is recompense and joy in itself.

* * *

There is a mysterious oracle in the book of Jeremiah: 'For God is creating something new on earth: the Woman sets out to find her Husband again' (Jr 31:22). The prophet means that, until now, it was the bridegroom, God, who searched for and pursued the unfaithful woman who followed idols. But a day will come when things will change. In fact, it will be the woman herself, the people of the new covenant, that will search for the bridegroom and hold him. That day has come! Now all this is fulfilled. Not because humanity has suddenly become wise and faithful, but because the Word took it to himself, in his own person, in a new and eternal covenant. The whole Good Friday liturgy is an expression of the fulfilment of this oracle. It began on Calvary, with Mary holding and kissing the face of her Son who had been taken down from the cross, and it continues now in the Church, of which she was in this case both the symbol and the first fruit.

The Church which, led by the successor of Peter, will now file past to kiss the cross, is the Woman who 'sets out to find her Husband again', who embraces him, full of gratitude and compassion, who sings with the spouse in the Canticle, 'I found him whom my heart loves. I held him fast, nor would I let him go' (Sg 3:4).

16

The mystery of the cross shines out

THE HEART OF the liturgical service we are now celebrating is the adoration of the cross, which will shortly
begin with the ritual of the unveiling: the pope receives
from the deacon a cross veiled in purple. Three times he
uncovers a part of the cross until it is completely revealed,
and the actions are accompanied by these solemn words:
Ecce lignum crucis, in quo salus mundi pependit: 'This is the
wood of the cross, on which hung the Saviour of the
world.'

To me, this ancient liturgical ritual is the symbol of the
mystery of the cross being gradually revealed throughout
the centuries. Each stage in the unveiling represents a
period of time, or a stage, in the history of salvation. The
first stage represents the cross as it was *prefigured* in the Old
Testament; the second stage represents the cross
accomplished in the life of Jesus, the 'cross of history'; and
the third represents the cross as it is *celebrated* in the
Church, the 'cross of faith'.

As we can see, the cross is present throughout salvation
history. It is present as a *figure* in the Old Testament, as an
event in the New Testament and as a *sacrament* or mystery
in the Church.

* * *

What did 'wood' or 'tree' represent in the Old Testament? It was the tree of life planted in the Garden, the tree of the knowledge of good and evil, around which rebellion takes place when human beings claim the right to decide for themselves what is good and what is evil. In the book of Deuteronomy the term 'wood' or 'tree' reappears, associated with a curse: 'One who has been hanged [on a tree] is accursed of God' (Dt 21:23). But certain passages introduce wood in a positive sense and these, in the light of what was later fulfilled, are seen as prophecies of the cross. Wood was used to build the ark that saved humanity from the flood; Moses used a wooden staff to divide the waters of the Red Sea (Ex 14:16); Moses threw a piece of wood into the bitter water at Marah to make it sweet (Ex 15:23 ff.).

What does the wood of the cross represent in the life of Jesus, in other words, no longer figuratively but as an actual reality in time and space? It represents the instrument of his condemnation to death, of his total destruction as man, the lowest point of his kenosis. The 'tree' (*xulon*), as the cross was often called, was the most infamous death penalty, reserved for slaves guilty of the greatest crimes. Cicero said that even the word was not to be pronounced in the hearing of a Roman citizen. Everything about the penalty was arranged to make it as degrading as possible. First the condemned man was scourged, then loaded with the cross (or at least with its horizontal beam) which he carried to the place of execution. There, he was tied naked and then nailed to this instrument of torture, where he died in agony, suffering convulsions and atrocious pain as the weight of his body pulled open his wounds.

'Crucified!': in the apostles' day, no one could hear the word without trembling with fear. And for the Jews, there

was the added element of God's curse: 'Cursed by everyone who is hanged on a tree' (Ga 3:13).

But in the light of the resurrection, what does the cross
represent in the age of the Church, according to what the
Spirit reveals about it through the apostles? The cross is
the place where 'the mystery of our religion' (1 Tm 3:16)
is accomplished, where the new Adam says 'yes' to God on
behalf of all and for all time. It is where the real Moses
divides the real Red Sea with wood, and by his obedience
transforms the bitter waters of rebellion into the sweet
waters of grace and baptism. It is where 'Christ redeemed
us from the curse of the Law by being cursed for our sake'
(Ga 3:13). The cross is the power of God and the wisdom
of God (1 Co 1:24). It is the new tree of life, planted in the
city street (Rv 22:2).

What was so decisive about what happened on the cross
to justify these statements? What happened was that God
finally destroyed sin, but without destroying the freedom
that produced it. He overcame sin, not by destroying it
with his almighty power or driving it out of his kingdom,
but by taking it upon himself, in Christ, and suffering the
consequences. He overcame evil with good, which is
the same as saying he overcame hatred with love, rebellion
with obedience, violence with meekness, falsehood with
truth. 'He was bearing our faults in his own body on the
cross' (1 P 2:24) He has freed us for all time.

* * *

This, in short, is the revelation of the mystery of the cross
as the apostles presented it. It was to continue in another
form (no longer as Scripture but as tradition) in the
Church. In a second-century homily, preached during a
Passover service similar to this one, a bishop introduced
this inspired hymn to the cross:

This tree is my eternal salvation:
On it I feed and there find nourishment.
Into its roots I sink my own,
along its branches I spread my arms,
its dew inebriates my senses,
its Spirit, like a caressing breeze, makes me fruitful.
This tree nourishes my hunger,
slakes my thirst, and clothes my nakedness . . .
This tree is my safeguard when I fear God,
my support when I waver,
my reward in the battle,
my trophy in victory.
This tree is the narrow gate and the hard road
    [Mt 7:13],
Jacob's ladder,
the way of the Angels,
at whose top the Lord himself truly is leaning
    [Gn 28:12–13].
        (*Ancient Paschal Homily*, 51 (SCh 27, pp. 177 ff.))

In the eyes of the Church the cross takes on cosmic dimensions. No longer is it just an event in history, but something that has changed the face of the earth. 'This heavenly tree', the same hymn continues, 'has raised itself from earth as high as heaven. It is the foundation of all things, the pillar of the universe, the support of the whole world, the cosmic bond holding unstable human nature together, securing it with the invisible nails of the Spirit, so that, once held, it shall no more break loose from the divine embrace.'

The account of St Andrew's martyrdom, which used to appear in the Office of his feast, tells us that the apostle, before stretching out on the cross, saluted it with these words: 'Hail cross, by which the Most High God has brought salvation! Hail cross, trophy of Christ's victory over his enemies! Hail cross, planted on earth but whose fruit is in heaven! Hail cross, whose name contains the fullness of all things! I know your mystery!' (*Acts of St Andrew*, in Lipsius-Bonnet, *Acta Apostolorum Apocrypha*, II, 1, pp. 54 ff.).

Christian art has made its contribution to this celebration of the mystery of the cross. The mosaics in the apses of some churches, such as Sant' Appollinare in Ravenna, show a large jewelled cross standing out against the background of a starry sky, and beneath it the words: *Salus mundi*, the salvation of the world.

* * *

In the year AD 569 the Byzantine emperor Justinian II sent a relic of the true cross as a gift to Queen Rudegunda in Poitiers. A Christian poet, Venantius Fortunatus, composed two hymns for the occasion, translating into song the Church's whole understanding of the mystery of the cross at that time. These same hymns accompany our service today. They have been used ever since by successive generations of Christians to express their heartfelt gratitude and enthusiasm for the cross of Christ. Through the communion of the saints, these hymns have come down to us imbued with all this wealth of faith and devotion. And that is how God hears them, sung to this great accompaniment, as by a single choir across the centuries.

Vexilla Regis prodeunt, fulget crucis mysterium: 'Abroad the regal banners fly, now shines the cross's mystery'. *O Crux, ave spes unica*: 'Hail to the cross, our only hope!'

The theme of the cross as the tree of life runs right through the second hymn:

Hail, true cross, of beauty rarest,

King of all the forest trees;
Leaf and flower and fruit thou bearest.

We shall shortly hear these words being sung: *Dulce lignum, dulces clavos, dulce pondus sustinet*: 'Fairest wood, and iron fairest/yet more fair who hung on thee.' Not even the theme of the cosmic cross is lost sight of: *Terra, pontus, astra, mundus: quo lavantur flumine!*: 'Their cleansing tide renewing earth and sea and starry sphere!'

At one point the poet addresses these moving words to the cross, as if to a living creature: *Flecte ramos, arbor alta, tensa laxa viscera*: 'Bend thy branches down to meet him,/bend that stubborn heart of thine;/Let thy native force to greet him/all its ruggedness resign;/Gently let thy wood entreat him/Royal sufferer, and divine.'

* * *

This, then, is the 'unveiling' of the mystery of the cross as salvation history unfolds. But it has to be renewed in every age. Today, the hidden power of the cross must shine out for our generation too. The ritual unveiling that takes place in the liturgy must be accompanied by an existential unveiling in the lives and hearts of each one of us. We read that the tree of life, planted in the middle of the new Jerusalem, has twelve crops of fruit in a year, one in each month (Rv 22:2). The cross has a harvest of fruit reserved for the present season in history, and we must try to gather it.

The question is: How is a society such as ours to understand the mystery of the cross, when it opposes the cross with pleasure at every level? A society that believes it has finally rescued pleasure and freed it from the unjust suspicion and condemnation that used to surround it? A society that sings songs in praise of pleasure, just as hymns were once sung in praise of the cross? A culture which is even called 'hedonistic' (deriving from *edonè*, meaning 'pleasure' in Greek), and of which, alas, we are all part to some degree, in fact even though we may condemn it in words?

Many of the problems and much of the incomprehension that exist between the Church and today's so-called secular culture originate here. We can at least try to get to the root of the problem and perhaps discover a basis for dialogue. The point we have in common is the realisation that in this life, pleasure and pain follow one another with the same regularity as a trough follows the swell of an ocean wave, pulling a shipwrecked person back into the sea even as he struggles to reach the shore. Pleasure and suffering are inextricably linked to one another.

Man desperately tries to separate these Siamese twins, to isolate the pleasure from the suffering. Sometimes we delude ourselves that we have succeeded, and in the euphoria of enjoyment we forget everything and celebrate our victory. But not for long. Suffering lies in wait, like an intoxicating drink that turns to poison on contact with the air. Not some different, independent suffering, due to some other cause, but the suffering that derives from the pleasure itself. It is the disordered pleasure itself that is turned into suffering. And this happens either unexpectedly and tragically, or gradually, due to the fact that pleasure cannot last, and because of death.

This is something human beings have come to realise by themselves, representing it in countless ways in art and literature. The inseparability of love and death, of *eros* and *thanatos*, was already known to the pagan Lucretius who says: 'A hint of bitterness arises from the very heart of every pleasure, which, even as it delights us, fills us with foreboding' (Lucretius, *De rerum natura*, IV, 1129 ff.). Even before the 'flowers of evil' have finished blooming, their singer himself assures us, they already smell of decay and death.

* * *

The Church claims to have an answer to this, the real drama of human existence. Why reject her explanation without once ever having really listened?

The explanation is this. From the beginning, human beings made a free choice, made possible by their composite nature. As a result, they came to direct their capacity for joy exclusively towards visible things, instead of aspiring to the enjoyment of God, for which the capacity had been given.

Through nature itself, God has linked pain and death to pleasure that is chosen against God and against reason (Gn 3:16 ff.), more as a remedy than as a punishment, lest by giving free rein to his selfishness man should destroy himself utterly, and each destroy his neighbour. We see, therefore, that suffering clings to pleasure like its shadow. But pleasure and pain do not compensate one another. The pain does not redeem the pleasure, being itself the fruit of pleasure, part of the same dialectic of sin.

Christ's cross has finally broken this chain. 'For the sake of [or, according to another possible translation, 'In exchange for'] the joy that lay ahead of him, he endured the cross' (Heb 12:2). He did the opposite to what Adam and every human being does, thus bringing a new type of suffering into the world: suffering that is not the fruit of pleasure and sin (purely passive suffering, as it were) but innocent and voluntary suffering. St Maximus the Confessor, one of the most profound Christian thinkers, wrote: 'The Lord's death, unlike that of other men, was not a debt paid for pleasure, but rather a challenge thrown in the face of pleasure itself, thereby changing, through this death, the destiny humanity deserved' (St Maximus the Confessor, *Chapters on Theology and Economy*, IV, 39).

But this was not the end. Christ is risen. The cross is swallowed up in victory. Christ has ushered in a new kind of joy, a new quality of pleasure – pleasure that does not precede suffering as its cause, but follows from it, as its fruit; that has its source in the cross, and there finds the hope that not even death can bring it to an end, that it is eternal. And this is true not only of purely spiritual joy but of every honest pleasure, including that experienced by a man and a woman in their mutual self-giving, when they generate life and see their own children grow, the pleasures of art, creativity, beauty, friendship and work well done – in short, of every kind of joy.

Only Christ can truly redeem pleasure and human joy from the sentence to which they were and still are subject. That sentence is due not only to sin but also to their very nature, which is corruptible and destined to die: 'The law of the spirit of life in Christ Jesus has set you free from the law of sin and death' (Rm 8:2).

The cross does not oblige us to renounce pleasure, but we do have to submit it to God's will, pursuing and living it in obedience to his Word and to the law which he has laid down. This he has done not in order to spoil our pleasure, but to preserve it from failure and death, so that through the small joys we encounter on our way we might learn to aspire to the joy that never ends.

* * *

The will of God is the 'cross' of pleasure. But if you should fall again, if you are not ready to accept the whole of God's will at once, remember that the cross is also a promise of forgiveness and mercy for those who fall. You are not expected to destroy yourself with guilt.

In Kafka's novel *The Trial*, the author tells the story of a man who is placed under arrest while going about his ordinary life and work. No one knows why. He begins the painstaking task of trying to discover the reasons, where the trial would take place, the charges against him, the procedures. But no one can tell him anything except that there really is a trial going on, and he is the defendant. Then one day they come to take him away for execution. It is the story of humanity struggling even to the point of death to free itself from an obscure sense of guilt which it cannot shake off.

In the course of the story we learn that there are three possibilities open to the man: he could either be completely acquitted, or apparently acquitted, or the case could be adjourned. But an apparent acquittal or an adjournment would solve nothing – the accused man would just be kept in a state of mortal anxiety for the rest of his life. On the other hand, if he were completely acquitted, 'all the records of the trial would have to be destroyed. Not only the charges against him but the trial itself and even the sentence would have to be cancelled from the record. Everything would have to be destroyed.' But no one knows if there has ever been such a case of total acquittal. There are only rumours, no more than 'beautiful legends'. Like all Kafka's works, the novel ends at this point: with something glimpsed in the distance, which you dream about but can never reach.

On Good Friday, we can cry out to the millions of men and women who see themselves represented in that accused man: complete acquittal *does* exist! It is not a legend, a lovely dream you can never reach! No. Jesus has 'cancelled every record of the debt that we had to pay; he

[150]

has done away with it by nailing it to the cross' (Col 2:14). 'Those who are in Christ Jesus are not condemned' (Rm 8:1). No more condemnation! Of any kind! For those who believe in Christ Jesus!

* * *

And so even today the mystery of the cross shines out: *Fulget crucis mysterium!* It is still a light for our path. Recently, a sociologist, writing about the current crisis of the Churches, said this: 'The Western soul is parched and withered. There is a *pantheon* open to all the gods, but it is starved of the sacred. Formal religion, social religion, the religion of good works, no longer speak to everyone. From deep within society, the need for a new contact with the divine is emerging, that will enlarge the soul and give people strength, joy, hope and a sense of life's glory' (F. Alberoni, in *Corriere della Sera*, 27 March 1995, p. 1).

This is precisely what the preaching of the cross achieved in the first ages of Christianity: like an uncontainable wave of hope and joy it swept away everything in which the people of the decadent Roman Empire sought refuge: mystery cults, magic, theurgy, new religions. There was a sense of a 'new springtime in the world'.

The preaching of the cross of Christ can do the same today, in this tormented age of ours, if only we are able to restore to it the inspiration, enthusiasm and faith of those early times. Recently, a European national Church asked an advertising agency for advice about how to present the Christian message at Easter. The reply it received was: first of all, do away with the symbol of the cross, it is too old-fashioned and sad! What a terrible misunderstanding!

What needs to happen is an 'unveiling' of the cross in the hearts of Christians, just as it happened in history and takes place in the liturgy. May we too pass from seeing the cross as a sign of condemnation and malediction, to seeing the cross as salvation, pardon, our 'only hope' and boast, until we can joyfully exclaim with St Paul: 'As for me, it is out of the question that I should boast at all, except of the cross of our Lord Jesus Christ!' (Ga 6:14).

The pope will shortly raise the cross above our heads. In the jubilee of the year 2000 he will also cross the threshold of the Holy Door carrying the cross of Christ before him. All this is the symbol of the Church which, from year to year, from century to century, from millennium to millennium, hands down intact to the world its most precious possession: the mystery of the cross of Jesus Christ. Truly, on this day, the mystery of the cross shines out: *Fulget crucis mysterium!*